PODCASTING FOR BERS

Learn how to Start and Grow your Profitable and Successful Podcast

By **David Toll**

Table of Contents

Introduction

You're totally in the right place if you're looking for a guide that explains how to start a podcast.

It is not hard to start a podcast but to get it started, there is a range of measures you would need to go through. There are also things you should know to make a good company out of podcasting here.

Podcasting is indeed an innovative new audio format that offers you the opportunity to listen to your choice of audio programming. People are making their own audio every day all over the world. Shows from music to technology and all in between on a wide variety of topics.

It becomes even more thrilling than distributing podcasting, simplifies delivering the message to the target audience.

What's more exciting is that, as it has been called, the Podcasting Revolution allows you to listen to, store, and enjoy this audio content whenever and wherever you desire. Perhaps not that, you also have the ability to produce and share audio shows with the ability to impact tens of millions of audiences worldwide on any subject you can envision.

We will discuss all areas of podcasting, educate you about its roots, and use the resources that offer the audience of the podcast the right to take the information they want anywhere they can take a portable media device. We also cover the equipment and software needed by a podcaster and provide alternatives for the participant on a strict budget.

This book has everything to do with podcasting. First, you know how to subscribe to podcasts and listen to them. Then you would learn how to develop, make, and promote a podcast. You will get a lot out of this book for both newcomers and established professionals.

1. PODCASTING: A FIRST INSIGHT INTO THIS BUSINESS

The word podcasting puts you in the right state of mind instantly. The central concept that stuck in my mind since I first heard the word 'podcasting' was a new, flexible communication medium with much to do with broadcasting. Podcast comprehension is on the rise. Podcasting as a platform is, like social networking a decade ago, on a journey to iniquitousness. It's a collection of data on the habits of the American media. It's awesome, and advertisers, like some people, love them for doing the research and making it accessible to everyone.

In homes, offices, cars, while driving down the sidewalk, in a park, and at work, podcasts are made. They may be orchestrated or unrehearsed, but podcasters often offer unaltered, genuine, as well as from commentary to their listeners. As a product tool, podcasting lets you meet hundreds of thousands of audiences. You don't have to think about federal legislation or licenses. You wouldn't have to worry about someone knocking your door down or buying a lot of gadgets. Podcasting has flipped heads since a very simple technical interface can be used to stream audio programming to which you subscribe instantly. What you downloaded is then automatically imported to Windows Media Player or Apple iTunes, and the audio file is then automatically uploaded to your phone media device. The best thing about podcasts is that your device isn't chained to you. Podcasting has evolved to an extremely powerful type of information that creates trust and loyalty from the little and misunderstood form of content. The success of podcasts has been boosted by podcasters and comedians such as Marc Maron and Joe Rogan, but now podcasts have everything. Podcasting can be an amazing marketing tool from a company perspective. It does not work for every company, but it can produce great results for those it does work: a new audience, more confidence and loyalty, and even more customers and sales. You wouldn't have to worry about someone knocking your door down or buying a lot of gadgets.

In essence, podcasts are an improved type of content: they are more entertaining than written posts, they (can be) evergreen, and, more than anything else, they give the listener a great deal of value.

Podcasting does not at all, at least not in the classic sense, use radio waves, transmitters, or receivers. As a distribution mechanism, podcasts use the World Wide Web, opening up a possible audience that may spread to the entire globe.

Podcasters create material that probably appeals to only a small group of listeners, as a general rule. Podcasts begin with an idea, something you have the desire and expertise to speak about, either actual or imaginary. Add a little push to that and an inability to accept no for a response.

The aim is to tell those who would like to hear what you want to learn.

Podcasts can be about anything, and just about anyone can appreciate them.

The subjects discussed don't have to be life-changing or earth-shattering. There are a couple of standard practice principles and guidelines, but there might be occasions when you feel that it is important to bend the laws. (That in itself can be a lot of fun!)

Over the years, podcasts have risen in popularity enormously.

They began as a misguided type of content (radio show, but it's not a radio show). Still, podcasting is increasing in popularity at a very rapid pace, and it is also growing trust.

Around 80% of podcast audiences connect to all, or much of each episode of the podcast and tune to seven shows a week on average. Perhaps one of the most popular podcasts is made by people who sit down every day.

They spend a few nights a week in front of their computers and just chat about their minds, hopes, and fears. Others have been focused on niche subjects; some are much more focused on broad subjects.

The leverage of podcasting for business has many major advantages:

Bring in a new audience: Via the iTunes Store and other podcasting libraries and resources, a decent podcast can help you get heard by people all over the world.

Create loyalty: As we have seen before, if you can get people listening to your podcast and enjoy it, then you have a loyal fan who will listen to all (or most) of your shows.

Formed trust: Podcasts will provide the listener with a lot of value. Beneficial tips and observations, interviews with people they meet and respect, etc., can be included. In the end, delivering real value is one of the strongest resources you have to create trust in your brand.

Draw customers to your company: One of the main reasons organizations should consider business podcasting is that it can be an awesome customer magnet. A great podcast that shows your understanding and abilities will help draw customers to you.

You will quickly find that there are podcasts about anything and everything: fictional podcasts, humour podcasts, parenting, children's podcasts, company podcasts, and so many others if you take even a few minutes searching through the iTunes Podcast Store or really any new system.

For a number of companies, podcast marketing may work, usually as an educational resource for their target market.

For instance, if you sell marketing software as a B2B company, you can develop a marketing podcast that teaches your audience how to execute those marketing strategies or with specific opinion leaders and influencers to discuss marketing techniques.

You can use podcasting to include advice about how to save money, how to spend your money, and so on, if you have a finance company like Ken Greene from earlier. If you have a cookie, chocolate, or cake business, well, you can use podcasting to share great recipes and explore techniques for cooking and baking.

Practically, there is a way to boost podcast marketing for almost every industry and use podcasting as a way to create trust, loyalty, reach a fresh audience, and expand your sales in the market.

What keeps you devoted to making your show would be your inspiration for podcasting. If your motivation is pure, you will be free to let your passion for the subject show through. In the end, it is your excitement that will "sell" your show. Please take a tough look at it before choosing podcast topics. Many popular podcasters make podcasts because they are deeply excited about their subject matter. They love it, whatever the subject is that keeps them going. There's a love for their show radiating from them. In order to produce the podcast they enjoy and can entertain/teach their audience, they will invest a lot of time and personal funds (to begin with at least). It's going to be too much work to generate the energy to do a podcast show week after week, and trust us; the show can never be a long-term success if there is no zeal and love for podcasting. If you are not persuaded of the subject yourself, so the audience will most certainly not be convinced either.

Is this podcast for me?

Podcasting turns the tables on schedules for programming, enabling the listener to have options on what to listen to and when, which makes it podcasts.

The ability to make an audio program transmitted through the Internet is not restricted to those with connections to a radio transmitter.

The easiest explanation for podcasting is that it's just pure fun!

Before you start a podcast, you must be explicit about why you want to start it. If you would like to start a podcast with the goal of making money, then it is even essential to pick the right topic.

The common ground that successful podcasters have over time is their connection with the audience. Listeners of podcasts are more likely to provide reviews on the podcasts they listen to than listeners of radio shows are likely to e-mail their views to the host of the show. The personal nature of a podcast is probably traceable to that. Podcasts offer more control, options, and intimacy to their listeners and makers than traditional broadcast media can.

The radio is, of course, much harder to talk to than a computer with an Internet connection and an e-mail. You are likely to get it, and from unexpected places, when you receive feedback. Since geography does not limit the distance your podcast can travel, you may find yourself in a distant land and foreign locations with listeners. And this feedback is not going to be always "Wow, a wonderful podcast!" They would be blunt and honest sometimes.

Why do you create a podcast?

Podcasts are already an unbelievably popular medium, as described above, and this trend is expected to continue. But they are also a rare intimate medium, developing communities of loyal listeners that are tight-knit. You get the opportunity to talk to a target audience about the things that concern you most, for what could be hours at a time. The lower entry barrier also suggests that podcasts cover the ground that TV and radio will never hit, ensuring that there is every possibility that you know or enjoy something that nobody else has recorded.

Undoubtedly, however, since you actually enjoy it, you can get into podcasting. It might not be for you if you don't like the thought of constantly chatting with a friend or two, putting in plenty of hours to edit the recording, doing the marketing, and holding up discussions with your audience.

However, for someone who has a creative flair and a passion, starting a podcasting company might be the ideal outlet and an exciting way to really enjoy your job for whatever it could be for.

One of podcasting's great benefits is its accessibility. In bedrooms and garages, many of the most popular podcasts have their origin as side gigs or passion projects by young newcomers and comedians who work. Anyone with a drive and some simple equipment can create a podcast and publish it, but that doesn't mean it's going to be a good one.

Podcasting has been a very saturated industry already. The average listener's time is minimal, with many podcasts lasting upwards of one or even two hours. It takes a well-realized idea to break in then, some forward planning, ambitious expectations, and the boundless energy to continue selling a product that might be slow to develop.

2. PODCAST IDEA: HOW TO DEFINE YOUR NICHE AND CHOOSE THE BEST IDEAS TO START

If you are clear about your inspiration to start a podcast, before finalizing the podcast subjects, getting the right idea about your audience is the next most critical aspect.

One question keeps coming up over again as people talk about podcasts and something they like about them. No matter what kind of podcast it is, it could be a talk show, a scientific podcast, a comedy show, a football analysis show. Rather, the listener will listen to something they relate to that is poorly produced instead of something with a high production quality but has no relation.

It is probably the most important factor to make your podcast a success with an honest link with your audience. You enter into an arrangement with them at the subconscious level when listeners subscribe to your podcast. In the expectation that you can bring value to their lives or entertain them daily, we agree to download your podcast on a constant schedule. This is a significant point; to maintain your part in this agreement, you must do your best. Skilled, techno-savvy individuals are podcast audiences. If you are sincere in upholding the trust then they have in you, over the long term, they will remain involved. Choosing a subject that fascinates, inspires, and excites you is crucial, and it will amaze, inspire, and excite others. Answers to these questions will mainly be determined by the podcast topics.

What is the platform from which you intend to make your podcast available? Android / iOS or otherwise.

Micro Niche Podcasts, subjects on Niche Podcast

Narrowing the emphasis on your subject will make the world today more satisfying. There are several common podcasts on current concepts that it will be a monumental challenge to get your podcast listened to and popular.

This is now the age of narrow casting/micro-niches or making available a podcast that can only cater to a limited percentage of targeted listeners overall. But, the appeal is immense for those to whom the software appeals. You have to realize that you will not be the first one! If you start a podcast on any subject today, then the chances are that there is already a really popular podcast on that subject or several popular podcasts on that subject. If you can identify your podcast's micro-niche and related audience, then chances are you will be much more oriented and generate qualitative content. You can build your podcast, learn the technique and expand your audience, then always spread to other related micro-niches and probably cover a complete subject.

Instead of beginning a large topic podcast, it is often easier to go deep into one tiny topic to start with and then concentrate on width. Even as podcast grows, the listener base grows, too. Soon, both listeners and podcasters can exchange stories, tips, and knowledge on that subject. A podcast that you figured only a handful of listeners would enjoy is essential to an entire audience when you pay attention.

Since about the beginning, and we are still having a blast, we continue to send messages to our worldwide viewers and challenge ourselves to create captivating media with new tricks and techniques. So, for the fun of that, well.

There are several prominent niches awaiting the introduction of a new podcaster. What attribute you add to that niche is more relevant than the niche itself.

When you contribute to the subject yourself, any topic you select will lead to the success of the podcast. If you are passionate about what you intend to talk about and can produce content day in day out on that issue, chances of success are much greater.

Names for Podcast: How to find the proper name for your podcast

You cannot judge the book by the cover, it has been said, but many people do that in order to make their decision, and it is imperative that they make it in your favour.

Podcast names are really hard to pick and can take a lot of time. At the same time, making the right first impression is important. Are the names of podcasts really important?

Actually, the answer is they seem to be. The name of your podcast and logo the first thing people can see when they come across your podcast, so if they don't like it, they're more likely to miss it and go to the next one. So, for your podcast to get some publicity, it is important to have a unique style and a nice logo. Note, people have never seen you before, they will judge your show by both the name and the logo, and it is essential to attract them with a nice design and a catchy name.

Often individuals beginning with a new podcast become so fascinated with choosing the right name that they most time end up spending a lot of time doing just that.

It feels like one of the most important decisions you would ever make while you are at the planning stage and choosing the correct name for your podcast. It can be very hard to make the right decision by having the right combination of clarification, imagination, scope, and information about the subject. But it is accomplished once it is finished. You need to just move on. There are different ways of selecting a good name for your podcast.

Using your Personal name for the show

There are several famous podcasts that have the host's name. However, in certain situations, the hosts are already famous or are already a celebrity via their blog or on a YouTube channel.

A brief overview of your show, followed by your real name, is also easier to have.

Something like: Carl Ryder needs company/companion/friend.

It may be a little hard to use the actual name to get the right first impression for anyone starting fresh.

Nevertheless, most podcast applications have a certain limit on the number of characters in the title. When choosing the title for your podcast, please be patient.

Regardless of whether or not you provide your name, and when you create a show, you already have provided the data for the author tag. They can always find your show if people search for your name.

Using your personal brand name

If you do have a blog or a YouTube channel and you are starting a podcast to promote the same sector, then it makes perfect sense to label the podcast with your brand.

You already have an audience, and communicating with them with the same brand name could be simple for you. You should not forget that the name of a blog and the name of a podcast are two separate items.

Name the podcast correctly, rather than using the same name, to represent your brand.

If you intend to host your own podcast, then it is also necessary to choose the right domain name. An optimized SEO podcast name would undoubtedly help you rank higher in the Google search engine while keeping your brand name

.

Using Inventive names for non-related podcasts

We may call them clever names for the podcast as well. You can choose a name that applies to the subject but has a slightly different meaning instead of explicitly criticizing the subject you want to speak about, or it may not have a meaning at all. Creative names are intended to sound sweet. If people associate your show with that name, then they will find it. It does not actually represent the subject exactly.

But if you are interested in the audience discovering you by doing research on Google or pod catchers, it may be hard to choose a creative name. For someone who is already recognized and already has an audience, choosing a creative name is simpler.

Suppose you want your target audience to check for you online. Better it is. Go commit to either a podcast name descriptive or keyword sort.

Form of Keyword podcast title

You cannot choose keywords for the sole aim of ranking on google and forget about the connectivity part. The title of the podcast must reflect on the subject you want to talk about. It needs to be relevant to your audience. So it should be imaginative enough, at the same time, to depict your personality.

Choosing keywords as a podcast theme may look too unnatural, and it may not be clickable by individuals. It is necessary to find the correct balance between the keyword nature of the title and authenticity. Google's search engine has evolved greatly, and search engine optimization is the norm of the day, and Google will find it if the content is nice and people like using it.

Descriptive type names of podcasts

This is the simplest choice for naming your podcast by far. What you're going to talk about, you can explain, and that will be it. Your title is simply that. The listener can quickly scan for descriptive podcast titles, and they can connect to them. They are not identifiers, but it may be a little hard to rank on the random keyword search on Google.

Descriptive names, however, usually rank better on a subject search, and this strategy can be a fruitful one because the search engines are heading towards semantic search.

Is it appropriate to use the word podcast in my title?

Well, each podcast used to have the name of the podcast in the title. This has become a stereotype, however. And over the number of years that the podcast industry is maturing, people have stopped doing it. Now that everyone knows that it is a podcast. So, using the podcast under your name is now quite pointless.

How to conclude at the correct name: What approach to pursue

The name of the podcast will only come to you in most situations, and it will just be perfect.

But if it doesn't happen, then there are some other ways of making a good name.

Thinking up names for podcasts

To come up with a podcast name, brainstorming can be used as a structured method. You can think on your own or with friends or inside your family. If you are a corporation, a group of workers may be interested in brainstorming.

You should get a sheet of paper with as many suggestions as you can scribble down. In the beginning, don't be too judgemental. Just go through the list of produced thoughts and think about what will be most important to the subject you're going to address?

A ranking strategy can also be used in more formal settings where everyone ranks their favourite names, and a cumulative score is used to pick the final name.

A funny or casual title can only fit sometimes.

Using a generator-name

You can try the transformer name, which could help you. Look for similar names for your podcast. Many online websites or podcast name creators are open. Only google it, and hundreds of them will be identified.

Get ideas for titles for podcasts.

Take inspiration. There are various ways you can get ideas from the name of your podcast. You should easily search for a few synonyms.

Are there any blogs that speak about the same subject or other podcasts that other people talk about? These places will help you come up with some ideas that are closer to your target name by a move or two.

You should check for books that may also throw up some great names on the subject of your podcast. But remember not to steal a concept from anyone else.

Are you desperately looking for podcast directories or niche podcasts? It is a great way to see and take inspiration from what other podcasters are doing.

Dos and Don'ts for names for podcasts

- A Happy Name

Make sure that with the podcast name, you get a cheerful, optimistic sound and a nice feel about your show. You should definitely throw back a boring, negative, or lame label.

- Avoid multiple copies

When you choose the name for your podcast, before you finalize anything, you can certainly Google it since there might also be another podcast by the same name. It is always challenging to waste a lot of time settling on your podcast's name and finding someone who already has the name.

- Avoid Resemblance

It can be a bad idea to even use a similar name to a previous name as the audience might become confused.

- Use your name correctly.

You must accurately use the name of your podcast and incorporate it into your logo, poster, podcast intro, and ads as well.

The correct name is the secret to finding your podcast.

If anyone looks for podcasts on a subject or topic, a list of suggestions will be shown to them. With the logo and episode titles, users can scroll through the list of podcast names.

It is, therefore, necessary to note what people will look for and link to the podcast title of the episode. It should not be keyword-focused and look like spam at the same time.

And while it is best practice to have simply and descriptively named content, it does not guarantee that you might appear at the top of any search engine results.

3. STRATEGY: HOW TO PLAN YOUR TALKS, SHOOTS, EDIT, AND HOW AND WHERE TO UPLOAD YOUR PODCAST

No marketer ever said, "I have far too much time and too much money," so it is fair to say that these days I am a pretty successful content creator I know, just put your jokes.

Your management teams are either contemplating or being pressured by all of you to consider making a podcast.

Stuff that you need to launch your PODCAST

Bunny Ferguson, Artistic Director with Jim and Trav of The Revolution Radio, highlights that you get what you paid for when it comes to gear. Let's be frank; everyone has experienced a poor podcast," she informed me. "If there is a failure of sound quality, if there is a lot of noise, static, scratching, or other noises in the background, it makes listening to it uncomfortable, and people prefer to turn it off. A lot of those issues are eliminated by getting good-quality equipment." According to Bunny, Jim and Trav have a very robust setup, although their podcasting package is not what anyone would recommend to someone just heading out."

Jim and Trav have been on the air for a long time, so I would call their setup the 'Tesla' for podcasters," Bunny also said. "Don't have Tesla capital, but still want efficiency?" Here is a suggestion from Midwest Outdoors Magazine and Midwest Outdoors Podcast editor Mark Strand: "I use my iPhone as a recording device to capture audio interviews of broadcast quality for podcast episodes, particularly if I am traveling. Rode, an Australian company, produces a smartLav+ lavalier [lapel] microphone and a fantastic little device, the SC6, which allows you to feed the audio signals from two microphones into a smartphone, as well as attach a pair of audio monitoring headphones.

If you download the company's free recording app, RodeRec, once you have the microphones (you can use your headphones to monitor sound), and you have everything that you need,' explained Strand. Mark steps it up with Final Cut Pro X for editing, which is used for both audio and video, as he often films during podcasting.

Digital files and editing are super easy to drop in. Your file should be converted to an mp3 for you by Garage Band, and then I suggest saving your completed podcast in a Dropbox account (free at http://dropbox.com). I Google the issue when I'm stumped on something and usually someone who has a YouTube video about what I need to understand. It would be great and insightful if you did the same sometimes.

As a novice, you definitely shouldn't begin pouring cash into podcasting apps. Because of that, while you are just getting started, most individuals would suggest free open source programs such as Audacity.

What is your PODCAST for?

So, first of all, why would you like to make a podcast? Are you a freelancer? A company? Or a leader in marketing? If so, you may have recognized podcasting as a great way to create authority and provide valuable and enjoyable material to your consumers and target audience. Or are you searching at podcasting from an enthusiast perspective? This could mean that in your spare time you will be making a show. And the topic would be something you are passionate about. You can describe your "why" here in either case. That's crucial to bear in mind so that even though you find it hard to get a show out, you can remain inspired. Next, what about your "who"?

Who is your audience?

Who are you making this podcast for? The thing is, you have no hope of building an audience until you exactly know who you're doing your show for and why you're doing it. If you come at it from a business point of view, and you are (for example) a personal trainer who wishes to make a podcast on health and fitness, then people interested in eating healthy, losing weight, fitness, or bodybuilding might be your target audience.

If you make a hobby show, let's say it's focused on your zombie love and post-apocalyptic fantasy, then your target audience will literally be people with the same enthusiasm. They may be fans of TV shows like The Walking Dead, Resident Evil video games, World War Z comics, and movies like Night of the Living Dead. A lot of intelligent people talk about building avatars or listener personas. It is a smart idea to sketch out just who you want your content to listen to.

"Each time you plan an episode, that persona is something to keep in mind: "Does Ken, our listener persona, like it? Is this based on what he's interested in, what he likes? The personality and those issues help you keep your show focused, all of which make for more engaging material. But how do you meet them once you know who you want to reach?

Pick a Subject

You want to concentrate your podcast on a particular subject or niche. Try to whittle it down to something that you can talk about for several episodes (100+), but it's not so wide that you won't appeal to your potential audience. For example, instead of making an "outdoor" podcast, talk about biking, or even more precisely, like biking for teenagers. As you become more popular, you can always broaden your topic later.

Do I need a crowd to start a PODCAST?

Before they launch a podcast, some people already have a bit of an audience in place. If you already have an audience centred on anything except your podcast, it's a perfect opportunity to lay the groundwork for the show's fan base. This may be anything from a corporation or brand to an artist, former athlete, or author. This, of course, means that your podcast is important to that audience. You can want to survey your audience during the planning phase.

Here, stuff like "what's your biggest point of pain?" you should ask them. "And what are you currently dealing with?" This may help you shape your material. You might even want to find out a little more about them. This can be anything from demographics and place to what other podcasts (if any) want to listen to. Just do not let this become a source of fear or "committee design"-you will begin to make some decisions sooner or later and press forward (preferably sooner).

The length of the podcast relies entirely on the material. Don't cut good content down or pad out brief jobs! To get the word out, how long does it need to be? If you asked some podcast listeners, a "short" episode would probably be under 15 minutes. And certainly, anything over an hour would be a "long" episode. Many point to the average commuting period (said to be around 20 minutes) to shoot for a good duration. But for an episode duration, anything from 20 to 45 minutes seems to be inside the "sweet spot."

Don't think too much about these numbers, though, and two factors can eventually determine your episode duration.

1. Material from you

2. Your viewership

Why cut it down to 20 if you have 50 minutes of valuable, meaningful content? Or, similarly, if in 10 minutes you've said all that you have to say, why pad it out to 30? Say that you interview extreme situations, and it's a great talk from start to finish, but it lasts for 2 hours. You can still divide it in half and make two episodes. With time, whether they think your episodes are too long or short, your listeners can tell you. To collect data like this, aim to survey your audience yearly, and you can change it appropriately.

There's no need to adhere to the same length each time when you get the information, of course, but it's nice to have an 'average' so that your audience knows what to expect. Finally, length can be a 'special' element, as we spoke about in Section 3. A certain type of listener might suit short and snappy 4-minute episodes, or enormous 3-hour in-depth interviews could suit another. Think about whether duration could be a particular, intentional option for you.

What if my podcast sounds bad

You can adjust some things if you feel like your audio doesn't sound as good as you would like. For instance, to get stuff that sounds closer to radio quality, you can use Audacity's compression and EQ settings. Multiple articles on their own may be the best way to use compression and equalizer settings, but this Podcast video offers a brief background on how to use them in Audacity.

You should have a website.

The question which should come to mind is: would you like to do this as a fun hobby, or would you like to do it professionally? You don't need a website if podcasting is more of a pleasure. However, you should certainly consider investing in a website if you want to create an audience, make money, and get acknowledged for your work. Money and time are the two big cons of a website. Enrolment and hosting of domains can cost money, but there are several ways to cut those costs and minimize the sum of money and time you spend designing and launching your site.

What way do you take from the website with so many different options out there? Well, there's Squarespace first, which offers consumers the option of creating a new domain name, using one of its many models, or trying out a website builder. For building a beautiful website, it is an all-in-one solution. Squarespace also has templates for Blogs & Podcasts that you can use and customize. Their Paloma prototype, for instance, is specifically built for podcasters. Wix is a platform that enables individuals to build, design, maintain, and improve their website, similar to Squarespace. In terms of templates built especially for podcasts, Wix has more choices than Squarespace.

They have a True Crime and a Safe Living podcast website design, for example. Squarespace or Wix could be the perfect choice for you if you search for an all-in-one form of solution. Then there is WordPress, which is fine to do whatever you want if you want total independence. WordPress has broad features, fantastic template designs, and advanced customization options, unlike the other two aforementioned options. The issue is that the learning curve can be very steep, and there is no specific support staff, just online guides and a platform, unlike Wix or Squarespace.

If you are not a designer for UX/UI, but you still want to build your WordPress website, you have two options:

Employ a designer

Purchase a visual page creator. Several front-end page constructors are available for purchase, two of which include Elementor and Divi. For the last five years, the writer of this article has been using Divi and is very pleased with its price point and usability.

How to guarantee that you have a good PODCAST interview

Let's be real, as much as we want to criticize other people for not bringing their A-game; it is up to us to take the first step as the producer of our podcasts and do what we can to have better interviews.

Stage 1: Build a checklist of "get ready to be on the podcast." This might seem trivial, but you might meet podcast guests who don't have a lot of podcasting experience. Recommend some easy stuff to them:

- Using Apple headphones as a minimum for the interview
- Check their connection to the internet or make sure they are in a quiet position with a strong internet connection.
- Closing all unwanted applications at recording time
- Close doors or turn AC off to prevent background noise

Stage 2: Give questions to your podcast guests ahead of time. Many people don't like to be shocked by questions; it can make a discussion really awkward. Send a professional email with a list of questions a few weeks ahead of time to make sure your visitor feels comfortable about the subjects you're thinking of exploring.

Stage 3: Separate from the interview, introduce your guest. One of my main pet peeves as a regular podcast guest is when a podcast host got me to introduce myself at the beginning of the broadcast. For the first 2-3 minutes of the episode, I give myself an awkward introduction (or worse, the guest gives me an awkward introduction, and I'm forced to be there listening to it).

There's a purpose why the most popular interview reveal that an introduction separates from the interview, and it's that when recording begins, it prevents any immediate awkwardness. Record your guest introduction AFTER the interview if you have an interview podcast, as it will give you a lot of contexts to share with your listeners.

Developing a campaign marketing

Users are shifting, attention spans are declining, and more folks are getting their content via mobile, which is why it can only benefit you and your podcast to have another touch point for your listeners. Before dipping your toes into the domain of social media, it is prudent to prepare a strategy that can be used to broaden and improve your podcast. Yeah, marketing can be enjoyable, but it should also have a very measurable effect on your overall aims and objectives. It is essential to reflect on where your potential audiences, such as topic-specific groups, Reddit, forums, or even Quora, spend time on and offline.

Go beyond the broad category of "podcast listener" and delve into your subject, whether technology, art, or relationships. As a subject pro, after all, you can also find yourself in several of these physical and digital spaces.

Editing and recording

Even simple GarageBand or Audacity acts can be very daunting if you haven't used editing tools before. It's easy to understand: audio production is full of vocabulary! If this is the case, Alitu may be the way to go. It's a tool for 'podcast making' that simplifies many confusing technical aspects and produces your episode for you literally. It's all right inside your browser, so there's no program to download, and it works on every internet-connected device. It is built to be easy to use and does just about everything:

- Takes control of clean-up of audio
- Allowing you to add music
- It helps you link your audio segments together
- Get your episodes directly distributed.

4. PODCASTING STYLES: WHAT THEY ARE AND HOW TO CHOOSE THE BEST ONE BASED ON YOUR AUDIENCE

Can your podcast entertain, provide data or teach someone? Is the age of your podcast dependent? Is it more likely that only individuals in a specific age group will listen to it? Is your position on the podcast dependent? If so, what location? Do you plan to draw both male and female listeners to your podcast?

This is known as listener analysis, so it will be very straightforward for you to pick the correct podcast subjects, structure, and design of your podcast if you have the correct idea about your audience profile.

The most successful way to lock down the story structure of your podcast is to plan it out before you start writing, and if the process requires longer than planned, don't get discouraged. When planning out the season's storylines for Breaking Brand, it took Buffer four passes before they found their angle.

Podcast Topics on selecting the subject of your podcast

For your podcast to start keying down on the topic. You can begin with a wide list of generic ideas or topics, or areas of interest first. You will be far closer to your final subject for your podcast after you have answered all these questions. You should talk with your friends and family members if you only end up having two or three subjects in front of you. Ask them what they'd like you to hear. What do they think you'll be good at?

You could also use a table with some parameters for decision-making and give scores against some of these parameters for each subject. An easy choice will be the one with the highest ranking.

To some listeners, it may reduce the prestige of your show to have no guests on your podcast. Unless you're a proven thought leader in your space, having your audience trust your word immediately is difficult.

To begin their show, some podcasters use a monologue or solo commentary, and then they move into an interview or panel discussion format. Like conventional radio and TV shows, they have produced a show with different segments.

Several interviews, music and sound effects, and heavier editing can require narrative-style podcasts. As a consequence, they are typically the most time-intensive format of the podcast.

You'll probably face a steep learning curve if you've never produced a narrative-style podcast before. Luckily, boutique podcast companies, freelancers, and podcast workshops are now available that can help.

If you think about monetizing your podcast in the meantime, then you might also want to throw in some additional criteria such as the subject's marketability, potential sponsors, potential affiliate marketing opportunities, the ability to develop info products or training courses on the same subject, your intended audience's buying power, etc.

There are several common niches for podcasting, but the one you like is the most significant niche. Many niches are kind of popular all the time because of the sheer size of the potential audience.

If and until you give the viewer something fresh and imaginative, the odds of success are very slim.

As in many instances in life, the best idea is to go with your gut instinct, go with your enthusiasm, no matter what method you pursue. Everything else will dynamically fall into place. All-time top podcasting niches, All-time most popular podcast subjects

1. Tech: Articles and talk shows and debates on general technology or items of technology. Tech podcast topics are very common, but they have a brief life and you need to come up with a large number of podcasts to keep your audience interested.

2. Personal Finance: Personal financial services, proposals for passive income, savings, selling, etc. Again, this is a competitive podcast niche, but it still has a great deal of potential as new players on this podcast subject are often accepted by the public.

3. News: All sorts of news, local news, or unique product or subject news sell more.

4. Sports: preparation for sports, tutorials, news etc. It's a very popular subject for podcasting, but it has a wide audience base. People enjoy and have a personal link with their sports. This makes it easy to manage the following and also creates a lot of possibilities in terms of affiliate marketing.

5. Self-improvement: Personal planning, personal development, psychology etc.

6. Inspirational: For many, a very normal and subject of personal interest. Wide scope for the promotion of affiliates.

7. Business: Corporate relations, launch of goods, etc.

8. History: Very common subject matter with a wide audience base.

9. Facts or fun facts: This is a sort of podcast subject where content will never be an issue and it should not be an issue for you to find new subjects to keep your listeners interested.

10. Stories: One of the most famous niches, science, thriller, fiction, crime, etc.

11. Comedy: Another one of the niches that is most difficult but still successful. But get into this if the audience is able to impress you. Making people laugh is a challenging art.

12. Culture: It's also a very popular podcasting niche, but depending on what you want to talk, it may have a venue, religious bias and can restrict your audience.

13. Music: A very popular podcasting subject, music is enjoyed by listeners of all ages and a music podcast dedicated to a specific genre can be a good starting point.

14. Animals: Animals and pets with no lack of content is once again a podcast subject.

15. Spirituality and faith could also be lovely when you have a deep understanding.

16. Politics: This subject requires you to be up-to-date with the latest details and unless you are going to share your opinions on current affairs, it is hard to master. It may also be contentious.

17. Relationship and love: Are you the type to give relevant advice to people in their relationship? This could be the best niche for you.

18. Games and banters

Subjects on Niche Podcast

Narrowing the emphasis on your subject will make the world today more satisfying. There are so many popular podcasts on controversial subjects that it will be a monumental challenge to get your podcast recognized and popular. This is the era of narrowcasting/micro-niches or making it available as a podcast that can only cater to a limited percentage of an intended customers overall. But, the appeal is immense for those to whom the software appeals. You have to realize that you will not be the first one! If you start a podcast on any subject today, then the chances are that there is already a very popular podcast on that subject or that there will be many popular podcasts on that subject.

If you can identify your podcast's micro-niche and related audience, then chances are you will be much more oriented and generate qualitative content. You can build your podcast, learn the procedure and expand your audience, then always spread to other related micro-niches and eventually cover a complete subject. Instead of beginning a large topic podcast, it is often easier to go deep into one tiny topic to start with and then concentrate on width.

As the podcast grows, the listener base grows, too. Soon, both listeners and podcasters can exchange stories, tips, and knowledge on that subject. A podcast that you figured only a handful of listeners would enjoy is essential to an entire audience before you know it.

There are several prominent niches awaiting the introduction of a new podcaster. What attribute you add to that niche is more relevant than the niche itself.

When you contribute to the subject yourself, any topic you select will lead to the success of the podcast. If you are enthusiastic about your topic and can create content on that subject day in day out, there are many more chances of success.

So, choose your niche and begin podcasting. It's all about continuity to build an audience. Consistency in the subjects you write about. Consistency on your blog in the format of photos. Consistency in the pace of when new content will be posted. And for podcasts, in your show format, continuity.

When they play a new episode, your audience likes to know what to expect. You'll find it harder to gain attention if your show features a serious interview one week, a funny debate the next, and a solo rant the week after.

When talking about it to other people, your listeners won't know how to explain your show, so it's going to be hard to get new audiences by personal recommendations. And if you start each week with a completely clean slate, it will be difficult for you to keep up with the development of content too.

It sounds like overhearing a discussion between two friends while listening to a conversational podcast. These types of shows usually have several hosts, and episodes could involve discussions on a concentrated subject (such as a Classic Vinyl album review table discussion) or a wide variety of items (i.e. they chat about tech, life, and the Internet on the media).

Such kinds of shows are simple to listen to, easy to capture, and seem to last from half an hour to an hour. Audiences will tune in just because they like the personalities of the hosts, and since it is a discussion they overhear, they will feel more related to the speakers than, for example, those who report a story in a non-fiction storytelling show. Such kinds of shows are simple to listen to, easy to capture, and seem to last from half an hour to an hour. The Negative aspect would be that:

You'll need to be imaginative and detailed with the subjects you explore in order to keep your audience interested and return for more.

You will have to deal with recording separately and editing the tracks together, based on where your co-host is situated.

And just as with interview shows, when you chat over Skype, you will be at the mercy of internet connections.

Think of the classic iceberg image. The recording is only one aspect of the process, and others may take longer. Altogether, you have to think about:

- Planning & Planning
- Set-up
- Writing notes
- Recording
- Editing & Mixing
- Uploading & Publishing

How do you pick the format of your podcast?

Ask yourself now that you've heard a bit more about the various podcast formats. What type of podcast would better suit my content?

If the answer doesn't come to mind instantly, here are some questions that will allow you to make the decision:

What do you need to get out of listening to your show with your audience?

If helping them understand is the main thing you want to do, then maybe an educational podcast would serve you best. Perhaps a conversation-based show with a funny co-host would work well for you if your aim is to entertain.

Whatever your aim, choose a format that is best to help you accomplish it.

How are you able to make your show unique?

Inside and format, there is so much space for innovation, and adding your own unique twist to it is vital. Interview shows, for example, are a common format in the company and marketing niche (for a valid reason, they allow the viewer to benefit from the experiences, achievements, and shortcomings of others), but this also indicate that you will have a lot of competition if you plan to start an interview show in this niche.

With is this common format? What are you going to do so that you stand out? Give your viewers a reason to listen to your show in your niche above the others. Maybe this may mean merging elements of two different podcast formats or presenting a different side of your subject that is not touched on by other podcasts.

Which format would suit your unique talents best?

Continue creating continuity by email with your audience.

Do you remember how we spoke in your podcast about your audience wanting consistency? Well, to hear from you, they will need continuity.

Let them not forget who you are and what you are all about in addition to selecting a layout that best suits your objectives (although, of course, you can always allow an expert to handle that aspect if you wish).

Keeping top of mind is important so that when they decide to learn about something, laugh, take a break from reality, or just listen to an interesting discussion, you can be the expert the audience looks at. And with email marketing, the simplest way of doing this is that as a podcast producer, getting an email list is important. Once you've got a new episode live, a product you want to pitch, or some sort of announcement you have, you need a way to directly reach your audience. What approach works better for you to determine whether you need an outline or storyline? A complete script and hours of planning time, or a single notecard and two mouse clicks, one for recording and another for stopping? Obviously, it solely depends on the personality of the podcaster, both methods work. It can be said that there is a very little difference between a writer and a podcaster: when putting together a short story or book, some authors tend to use an outline; others only take an idea, a few points, and a guide, then let their fingers work all across the keyboard. Many podcasters plan for podcasts in the same way as professional meetings, including podcasters emerging from corporate offices. To keep the podcast on track, they make notes of key points on note cards, but the points are the only material they compose beforehand. From workplace to podosphere, you can quickly apply your organizational skills.

C.C Chapman, for instance, in his day job, he feeds, breathes, and sleeps. Based on a few bullet things, he was able to take this "PowerPoint mentality" of talking for 30-60 minutes and applying it to his show. His whole preshow training for his handling the Gray podcast is to take suggested subjects or questions from the audience, jot down a few bullet things, and run with it. He starts his one-take recording with a couple of points acting as a guideline with a selection of ideas and subjects compiled between podcasts.

The Evel Knievel's of the podosphere are simply some podcasters, firing up their microphones and recording in one take. These podcasters appear to have music and entertainment backgrounds, determining when a change in delivery is needed in a brief moment time.

This is a fast-thinking talent, and while it keeps the content spontaneous and fresh, it is a talent that needs to be established over time. For instance, the crazed mind behind the sharp and sarcastic podcast, The Bitterest Pill, is Dan Klass. His show is developed entirely. Time for no prep. Not a list insight of main points. Exactly how he got it done is with this special courage that he has grown with over time.

Dan is a talented stand-up comic. For a significant number of podcasters, excitement is a driving force that holds their podcasts spur-of-the-moment. They keep their preparation time to a minimum with ample drive, motivation, and trust in their message because podcasting is not a chore but a means of recreation.

Timing in Podcasting

Time, the most precious asset we have, is all about it. The only other one from which we just can't gain more! So, let's get started: How long does it take to create an episode of a podcast? And here's what I have for you:

1. The Period that You Have

One can spend as much time as you deem fit on podcasting. Find out all the alternatives here.

2. Variables

Here's what decides how long it takes to do podcasting and how to keep the time down.

3. The approaches

Three different methods of podcasting, and the time needed for each one.

There are several podcasts running for less than ten minutes where hosts deliver their message and then sign off just moments after you thought they were signing on. On average, a podcast runs from 20 to 30 minutes per episode, and this is more like an understandable average, not necessarily a scientific, comprehensive analysis of all the podcasts out there.

There really are five-minute podcasts that cater to a certain form of audience and four-hour podcasts that provide a specific topic with in-depth coverage. The daily podcast appears to be 20-45 minutes, usually the same duration as the typical commute. Figure out what works for you, and where appropriate, and do not be afraid to modify the duration.

Avoiding Noise and external disturbance during your podcast

You will discover that traffic is lighter at night or early in the hours of the morning, children are in bed, staff are not running jackhammers, animals are normally less busy, all adding up to less ambient noise, so the microphone takes over.

Stuff towels underneath the handle. It reduces the amount of sound that filters into your recording area from inside your home. Hold the microphone as far away as possible from your machine. The fan (if loud) actually becomes part of the podcasting room's normal ambiance.

Turn off any ceiling fans or additional air conditioners or extra heating systems

Ionizers in rooms. With fewer devices running, you have less chance of additional noise. Simply give it a few moments if you encounter ambient noise that you don't want in your podcast. Wait till the noise subsides, pause, and then, a few lines before the interference, pick up your podcast. That is indeed for the sake of post-production: You can easily narrow down where your edits are needed with a significant gap in your podcast activity.

How much time have you got?

Podcasting will take as much time as you make it. The variety of podcasting types, formats, and quality of output is as wide as the number of podcasts in the universe. There are individuals out there who spend weeks making only one episode of 20 minutes.

Then there are those that in 20 minutes, plus the time it takes to hit record, stop and upload, knock out everything the same length.

What you wouldn't want to do is stretch content to match a rigid timeline or, on the other hand, jam so much data into an episode that listeners are overwhelmed by it. A podcast's aim is to communicate with listeners and build a network over time. People will spend their time listening to what you have to say, because they will make it worth their time.

How often you continue to release episodes will be dictated by your content. If you're trying to create a brand or gain momentum with a following, though, consider recording and publishing an episode every week.

Creating a few episodes before you launch does the trick to stop getting frustrated and hurriedly generating new episodes. You may not feel unnecessarily pressured in this way, but you can also adhere to a daily or weekly schedule for your audience and subscribers.

Often times, podcasters begin by saying that a given set of shows per week will be created only to discover later that they cannot keep up with the pace. Quality broadcasts would be enjoyed by your listeners against the amount. When most of us started, we thought we would do three shows a week and found out that that form of dedication was not matched by our schedule.

Questions you may want to consider

How many shows would people want to listen to every week?

1. Just how many shows with the same theme are being produced?

2. Is there enough new material I can find to support the number of shows I want to create?

3. Can my plans suit my budget based on what I now know?

4. Within the constraints of my family, can I build the content?

5. Without affecting my work, can I build the content?

6. When a team member is not present, can I create a show?

What are 10-minute monologues like? Some people may ask if the size and time matter. Is there such a thing as making a podcast too short? Here are some benefits of delivering a simple and short podcast:

Shorter production time: Production time could be reduced from preparing, speaking, recording, and mixing for a week-long project to a single afternoon. With a fast and straightforward production schedule, it's easier to produce a podcast on a daily basis, such as every one week, daily, or twice a week.

Quick downloads: You can be confident that your podcast listeners will still have fast and reliable downloads, no matter what specifications you compress your audio file down to.

Simple to remain on track: You force yourself to adhere to the purpose (and the actual message) of your podcast if you restrict yourself to a running time of fewer than ten minutes. There is no space for the exploration of in-depth chat, spontaneous banter, or tangents. You press the red button and stay on track from start to finish, keeping your podcast based solely on the facts. Upon reading your show notes and descriptions, you should be able to figure out your show's estimated running time. Some podcasts can probably accommodate up to two or even three hours on a given topic. Even ardent podcast listeners will want to sit and wait for such a mammoth download, it's difficult to imagine, but massive productions have some definite benefits:

If the show is an interview type, you have power for anywhere from two to four hours. Discussion going beyond the 30-minute mark encourages you and your co-hosts or guests to move out to loosely connected banter, expanding the focus of your podcast and stimulating debate that can proceed in other directions. Be vigilant about this one. Shows and interviews that ramble aimlessly run the risk of losing the attention of the listeners.

Now that you understand a few of the styles of podcasts available, you can start making a more informed decision about what kind of style and format of podcast fits your podcast's ultimate goal. Are you trying to communicate? Great pleasure? Amuse? Depending on your response, the format will change, and the style of voice you choose to adopt will change as well. Listening to different podcasts as possible and having an idea of the style is the best way to decide the vocal qualities of the host and the style in which they present data.

Starting to wake up

Almost every guru of success, visionary leader, and coach, and so on advises that you wake up earlier than normal. It's good common sense, for podcasters in particular. You're less likely to have to compete with leaf blowers from other folks. Some people probably haven't broken into your brain, either. It's an ideal time for sound mixing or recording. If you scheduled your alarm five days a week, half hour earlier than regular, you've earned yourself an additional 2.5 hours of time per week to work on your podcast.

However, the majority of people fall into unique categories. It relies on priorities, skill and your background. The balance you're comfortable with between the times spent and the resulting output really comes down to it.

Organization

Organization is the simple act of coordinating everything that is necessary to complete your podcast. Someone who runs an interview show is the most obvious example here. A fair share of time needs to go into locating, investigating, calling, negotiating and scheduling interviews while you're interviewing. Then you have messages to use around the mic, the material to cover, and far more. The organization that goes into doing an interview show is not underestimated, it's not insignificant.

Coordinating with co-hosts, coordinating meet and greet times or finding rooms to record in may be other aspects of the organization. You're beginning to see that these aspects are really reliant on the structure of your show and how you set up your episodes.

The best thing is, of course, that means that you can pick your format based on how much time you have. If you're very time constrained, don't do interviews. They appear to go longer, coordinate a lot, and still need a good bit of preparation. Do a solo and chat about what you know well for the shortest recording possible time. And, at a moment's notice, you can knock out a 15 minute episode with little organization and just a bit of planning.

Planning

The preparation process is entirely human, and there are as many methods as there are podcasters. You can find your own way, but it appears to fall on a range that is pretty well defined.

You have people on one end who think up a topic and just start talking. That works well for far more conversational co-hosted shows, and the hosts know the subject inside-out.

You will find hosts on the other end who create a complete script for their broadcast, including plots, interview segments, co-hosted features, so every part of the episode is carefully prepared.

Before writing up a fairly comprehensive bullet point, outline on what they want to discuss, you will find other people who spend 30 to 45 minutes doing a little research. You can also find those who only spend 5 minutes jotting down top-level talking points, maybe 5 to 10 bullets that each trigger a few minutes of conversation.

Configuration

By setup, we refer to equipment and IT. This involves all the time you spend taking your microphone out, plugging it in, launching Skype, and then figuring out your audio settings before a session. It also includes checking the mixer, setting the levels, and preparing the digital recorder, among a million other items, if you're on a more complicated system. It involves doing the reverse after the recording, packing it away again. Then, get your PC out, fire up the editing kit, and get started.

Depending on the background, setup time varies. Can you find a room where your machinery is permanently set up? Do you also have a desk at home where you can have your microphone, always prepared to go, mounted on a boom arm? That could save a great deal of time. But, for many, it isn't practical.

Types Of Podcast

Interview Podcast

The advantages of podcasting an interview are:

- This will open up the show to a new audience

If your guest posts the episode they were on through their social media pages, they open up a whole new set of ears to your podcast. For those who want to make a podcast where they get to know a subject they are not already an expert in, interview podcasts are a great option. Some are personally recorded, but many are remotely recorded, which means that recording the initial episode would only take about one hour to two of your time.

Whenever you're thinking about the atmosphere you want to build for your guests, keep that in mind. And if they had a nice time, individuals would still be more prepared to share your episode. This is typically the first format people think of when they hear the term "podcast" because of the popularity of creators like Joe Rogan. This style is also possibly the easiest to make, given that you can get good guests.

- This gives you access to more diverse content.

An interview show opens your podcast up to diverse perspectives, stories, advice, and experience instead of taking sole responsibility for the last piece of content. This gives the audience a lot of variety and takes a great deal of pressure off you.

- You can do this from the convenience of your very own home

All you need is a machine, a strong microphone, Skype; then you're ready to go. It also allows you more options to record your podcast remotely with guests, which means you may be able to draw foreign guests, and that's always a positive thing.

The downsides of podcasting an interview could include:

- Reservation of visitors can be hard

It could be hard sometimes to get guests to commit to coming to a show they have not been aware of or that has no following or an established reputation while you're starting out. That doesn't mean it's difficult, and all you need to attract the next guest is the first guest.

However, if you're hoping to start your show soon, this is something to keep in mind. To have a good amount of content, it could take a while to get enough guests locked in.

- You have to work with the schedules of other people. It can be difficult to find a moment to capture, especially if you're trying to book someone who is very busy. This is why you need to be versatile. You have to navigate around them if you're a newbie podcaster and you want individuals to come to your show for free (which would be the norm).
  - If they share their episodes with their fans on social media, your guests will help you expand your audience. For this podcast style, all you need is a system, a recording, and a microphone, so there's no need to be a technological genius.
  - Work takes a lot of time to complete.

If you're well prepared, the guest will always be more open and generous. Unfortunately, it consumes a lot of effort to be well trained.

It's always best, as a general rule, to have new interview questions for each guest you put together through analysis.

But it could get boring if you don't do it right or if it doesn't suit your content when doing your show this way, it will minimize preparation time.

- Your destiny is in the hands of your guest.

Often, on a bad day, you get your visitor, or you ask a question they don't like, or they simply don't like you, maybe. These items will always be out of your control, but the only way to prevent this is to be as prepared and enjoyable as possible. If you have something curly to ask, it's also a good idea not to bring those questions at the start of your interview. And, you may perform a pre-interview so that it's not when you're seated in front of a microphone that you first meet your guest, try to arrange an additional 10-15 minutes before the interview if you can't do a pre-interview so that you can get comfortable with each other. It's always best, as a general rule, to have new interview questions for each guest you put together through analysis.

But it can get very uninteresting if you don't do it right, or if it doesn't suit your content when doing your show this way, it will minimize preparation time.

For good material, you're absolutely dependent on visitors. So if you catch them on a bad day, the episode will suffer as a result, unless during the interview you can turn it around.

For interviews, editing doesn't have to be absolutely perfect. Instead of seeming out of place and confusing, all the "uhms and arrgh's" would be part of the normal discussion. If you would like to polish things up, you can still edit these out, but it's not necessary. This is an incredible time-saver.

The Podcast on Solo

This is a fairly popular form of a podcast and is mostly used by individuals who have information that they want to discuss with an audience in a certain field.

If more individuals listen to podcasts, more individuals may want to make their own. You'll just have to decide what kind of podcast you're going to make unless you're one of those people. Will you be interviewing people? Are you going to tell stories of people in your business doing awesome stuff? Perhaps you just want to audibly rant online.

Solo podcasts often appear to lack audio diversity, as it is just a single voice, which can lose an audience's interest. Additionally, because you're speaking for the vast majority of the show, you will have to do multiple takes.

This podcast is not difficult to pull off, from a technical viewpoint. But holding a microphone on your own is tougher than you think. Without making a fool of themselves, it takes a special kind of individual to continue a monologue about any length of time. You don't have to ad lib, of course, all those stuffs that many podcasters do, and you can just write it all out. Then, the trick is to write and read the script as if you were conversationally speaking. Podcasts are not like audio books in fact, listeners don't expect someone to hear them reading. They want to hear somebody's talking.

At the other hand, the setup is just you, a microphone and your audience listening. The benefits of a solo podcast include:

- You don't have anything else to think about

Since you're traveling alone, without thinking about having to lock up a guest or co-host, you can work on your own schedule.

- It is easier to edit

It's much better to edit one voice than to edit multiple voices. Plus, you have the added joy of not having to deal with stuff like talking about things that can be a pain to cut around in the ass.

When you appear solo, you're much more likely to remain on track and stick to your episode schedule, and that's always a positive thing.

If you screw up a line, no issue, just say it again and edit the repeats, you can spend a lot of time as much as you desire in recording each episode.

- This is a perfect way to build your own personal brand.

It is a good way to develop yourself as an expert in your field to do a solo show so you can share your experience with an audience.

Conversely, it's a perfect way to get your perspective out into the world if you're a comedian or social critic, without having to write a whole comedy festival show or get a spot on TV or radio.

- You will establish a deep relationship with your audience.

It's just you and your audience as the host of a solo podcast, so it's a lot easier to establish a bond with them quickly.

It won't take long for your audience to feel like they know you, because you're talking directly to them, not to a co-host. If they start feeling like that, they're more likely to hang around AND suggest your show.

The drawbacks of a solo podcast are:

It's hard to get the resources right up there,

It can be hard to harness the conversational energy you need to keep an audience involved if you have no one to bounce off.

It's quick to go off on long tangents if you're not planning your episodes. You should be careful not to sound like you're reading something out in a monotonous voice if you're scripting it out. To strike the perfect balance, it takes practice. This is much more complex than it seems.

So, whether you're brand new to podcasting and nervous behind the mic, before going live, I would suggest taking time to develop yourself so you can get as relaxed as possible. Spend time listening back to your shows, too, so that you can figure out just how much energy you need to make your program sound exciting. Notice that there is no time limit for this. Before you announce something and no one ever wants to know, you might be recording practice episodes for years. So, practice, workout, practice and you're going to get there.

Display of the panel

This type of podcast is also perfect for shows like NPR's 1A in the news/current affairs format. It requires a little more work to produce a panel podcast. First, whether you are all in the same room or not, everybody should have a microphone.

Second, when it comes to recording several various sources of sound, there are some technical obstacles to jumping. Third, to find a day and time that everyone is available to record could be a hassle.

It is composed of a host and a number of guests who rotate each week (often experts).

The Benefits of a show on a panel

For your audience, it keeps things interesting. Every week, a panel show is a perfect way to give the viewer's something fresh because they have constant access to new views and perspectives.

- The content pressure is removed from you

You have got other people to rely on for content because you have other minds in the room.

Yeah, you're going to need to moderate a discussion, that can be hard work, but you're going to get so much more from your guests, too, than you're going to be able to dish out on your own.

The Downsides of a show for a panel set up are:

- Booking guests can be challenging.

Not only is it complicated from a planning perspective, but it might be hard to get guests to agree to come to your show if you are starting out. It doesn't mean it that's unlikely. In reality, you can draw on your personal connections if you work in an industry where you have a lot of colleagues who would provide great insight into your niche.

The problems aside, this format has some real benefits. Throughout the panel, the responsibility for being fascinating is distributed. If the energy among the panel members is strong, it is always interesting to listen to a conversation between some opinionated individuals.

You don't have to follow any of those formats for a pure form. Mixing and mixing! Have a little fun! We have so many podcasters out there who combine various elements of these types to produce their broadcast.

Do not forget that the more individuals you engage in your podcast, the more time it takes to wrangle certain individuals. If you have a lot of producers working behind the scenes, that's great, but if it is just you, doing this on top of working a full-time job can be more trouble than it's worth it.

- Keeping things on track can be challenging.

To keep a show such as this going and advance the discussion from guest to guest, you have to be very professional as a moderator.

Often you will have panel members who will step in automatically after everyone is finished. They may need to be spoon fed at other moments. Either way, it's your responsibility to be on top of things and keep the conversation going.

If you do this with individuals in different places via Skype, it can be hard to get the rhythm right. But if you hit it, it might sound fantastic.

Podcasts that are conversational and co-hosted

This style is very common and two or more people, sitting around, shooting the shit, are the basic set up.

There would also be one person who takes care of the show's business, such as presenting the show, setting up the subjects, and listing the calls to action at the end. Every week, get together with a pal or two and record your conversations. This is all that there is to it. This is great for those who want a podcast that is fun to create with little effort. If you have someone who's interested in the same subject as you and who you'd work well with behind the mics, this format is perfect. The Main advantage of podcasts that are conversational and co-hosted are:

- This is a fan favourite.

These are the shows that develop fans very quickly if you have great chemistry with your co-host(s), so people want to be part of the club.

These shows are often characterized by listeners as "keeping up with old mates."

- The prep and preparation work can be divided between you.
- These are also the most enjoyable to do - a good and engaging co-host and some interesting discussion points to discuss are all you need. If you've got good chemistry, this format will turn into a fan favourite. Listeners will feel like friends are catching up.
- It's fun to have

This type of show can be an absolute blast if you have excellent co-hosts who make you laugh and continually surprise you with their thoughts and viewpoints.

- Relying on others for material or content

When you come up with material for a weekly broadcast, two or three heads is better than one.

Planning can be a creative dream if you've got co-hosts who carry a lot of ideas.

This style of podcast is fantastic. It's a wonderful live show that makes sense if you want to go out on the road and do your show in front of a live audience.

It is much better to edit one voice than to try to edit several voices all talking about each other. No need to stick to the timetable of someone else or run ideas past someone else. You have full creative power, and each episode can be approached as you see fit.

Disadvantages of podcasts in conversation is that:

- They all need to be on the same page.

The more you have co-hosts, the further you are at the whim of the preferences, priorities, and lifestyles of people. So, everyone needs to be 150 percent on board to make this a success or the show will inevitably fizzle out.

A relationship with a podcast is like a marriage, because you have to select the right and correct person or individual to get to bed with.

- It's more difficult to edit

The more participants you have on your podcast/show, the much more potential you have for over talk, tangents, fuss, and hype.

If you haven't got a lot of time for editing and post-production, this is important to remember.

Also, recording less audio is a smart idea because you don't want to try to whittle down three hours of recording to a 30-minute broadcast. Other drawbacks could be that only the hosts and their mates are involved in these podcasts. It can be very difficult and stressing to keep audiences entertained if you and your co-host aren't experienced comedians.

Insider jokes and references that listeners won't understand / think about are easy to make. At all times, you need to keep them in the loop.

Material Recycled

Another common way of assembling your podcast is to repurpose content. The material available in podcasts in 'repurposed format' varies from lectures, conferences, other interviews, etc., and it can really help to enrich the experience of the listeners. You'll see a lot of TV shows do this where they're going to repurpose their TV show into a podcast for individuals to catch up later on.

Perhaps you are interested in a live show that would perform beautifully as a podcast and there might be a chance? Editing would also be needed since the live show will seldom be put out as a podcast in exactly the same way as it was carried out on stage. If the material converts, however, it can be a perfect way to get two samples out of the cherry content.

The Moth is a common example of a form of podcast which uses repurposed material. The podcast presents the best stories that have been shared on stage from all over the United States each week. The Moth is capable of assembling these stories because The Moth's own listeners send the stories and audio files. Themes vary from personal and social backgrounds, as well as other stories that are culturally significant.

Form of Narration

Anyone who gets up on stage to tell their own unique tale is a listener of The Moth. The speaker is also the audience. In this context, the podcast does a very real job of forming human ties between the listeners and the podcast speakers. A unique way of engaging and attracting audiences is this form of podcast. Here, no surprises.

The most successful way to lock down the story structure of your podcast is to plan it out before you start writing, and if the process requires longer than planned, don't get discouraged. When planning out the season's story lines for Breaking Brand, it took Buffer four passes before they found their angle.

The narrative style is more engaging. The topic is much more like a conversation you would have with your friends, even though podcast is broken down into different parts. The hook for the audience is that it makes the format sound like you are listening to a group of friends and their views on different political issues

.

Non-fiction podcasts on storytelling

This style of podcast can be very hard to do well without a big team of people supporting you, even if you're an accomplished podcaster.

This model also includes a team of journalists, writers, producers, sound designers, as well as a lot of time.

You can create stories like this as easy or complicated as you like, but there are also a lot of audio components, like interview recordings, ambient music, telephone calls, audio behind the scenes, the list goes on.

So if you don't know what you're doing, that's a style I would have stopped in the early days.

Storytelling podcasts for fiction

While more individuals are hopping on board, this is a less crowded room than non-fiction.

This can be a perfect way to get your writing out there if you are a good writer, but again, it needs more than just speaking into a microphone.

This style includes music, production and possibly a voice-over artist, and is more audio cinema than audiobook version.

Multiple hosts

This can function as one super host; they can bring to the table more perspectives, insights, and questions. The workload of one podcast can also be shared by your hosts, making life a little easier. For instance, if you have two guests on an episode, instead of just one host interviewing both, each host can interview one guest.

Creative decision-making and air time on a co-hosted podcast, which are two of the most rewarding and motivating parts of being a podcaster, can be difficult to balance.

In order to keep the episode on track, you also need to find the right balance between co-hosts digressing that the crowd enjoys and dialling things back.

To stop these cross-talks and digressions, you will probably also have to spend more time in post-production.

Upon that, notify your guests well in order to ensure that with fantastic interviews you can fill your calendar. This will create a sustainable pace and also allow you plenty of time to advertise guests in advance and highlight them.

In addition, connect on your own to the podcast, take notes on how well the other host manages the episode on track, and make your co-host do the same. During your one on one meeting, you will use these notes to strengthen your hosting and interviewing abilities. This gives a new perspective on your respective performances and encourages you to work together to strengthen your show.

Transforming your podcast into an enterprise

It doesn't immediately turn you into a businessman to start a podcast, and your podcast company won't build itself. Though if you take it seriously, and it continues to build an audience, your podcast can naturally turn into a company you're going to need to take care of.

When you start to incur costs (e.g. facilities, studio costs, travel, software), and when the income from sponsors, live performances or external revenue sources (e.g. Patreon) allows it a living rather than a hobby, the best way to say when you need to formalize the process is.

At this point, to secure your assets, and profit from more favourable tax rates, you will probably want to incorporate a business around your podcast. This will also help you formalize relationships with your contributors, either by hiring them in an official capacity or by sharing company leadership.

Given the potential of podcasts to attract and retain an audience, it is no wonder that business owners, entrepreneurs and advertisers are looking to capitalize on this medium's success.

As a podcaster, in a specific subject or area, you can position yourself as an expert that will help you influence consumers and clients in ways that inspire them to buy your goods and services, invest in your company, or promote you to their peers. And all of it can be accomplished on the cheap, since producing a podcast does not involve a major financial investor in most cases.

Editing and Production

Bad decisions elimination

Editing is where a lot of hours are lost by amateur podcasters. This is motivated by two factors: trust and perfectionism. When you're recording, have the courage to make a mistake, and instead of repeating the segment, just laugh, correct yourself and move on. When you trip on a few words, or make the wrong decision, no-one cares. Only make fun of it and proceed. You achieve two things if you take a perfectionist mentality and plan to edit every last one of these:

First, you get nervous about yourself, leading to even more fluff.

Second, you set yourself the arduous task of editing details, which implies listening through lots and lots of the show, exponentially increasing production time.

There are strategies to make editing simpler for major errors that you just can't get rid of. Suffice it to say, the aim is to reduce post-recording edits to virtually nil. The errors are okay, they make you sound human. Sorry, repair it, move on and leave them in.

Music & FX

You might also want to edit audio, sound FX, intros, outros, interviews, excerpts, and on and on, in addition to the elimination of errors! These add variety and can improve your show's efficiency, so they are always worth adding. But audio, as FX and bumpers do, adds editing time. Even adding an interview means that you have to piece a few components together, thereby adding time for editing. Many great shows have shunned some sort of musical fancy and it's never affected them. To reduce editing time and contribute to the sustainability, keep it as easy as you can.

The Publishing

Publishing is all that occurs after the final audio files are created by you. This involves making the page for your episode, inserting show notes, uploading your media file, and any advertising of the episode you want to do.

Perhaps, there is a balance you might spend hours writing extremely informative show notes, publishing a complete transcript and then advertising the show to every man-known network. But, it's just going to mean that you're already working on that next week when you need to film your next episode.

Promotion is an art in itself, which wouldn't be explored here, but a short discussion is worth showing notes. Some prefer to keep it straightforward, only listing a few links listed during the show. Others put up a lot of content, making a companion blog post for the audio episode, really. To the listener, the former serves its function, but very little.

The above implies that you add value to your website and make it more likely through the quest that people are going to find your content and thus be guided towards the episode. That, of course, will win your listeners over.

Choose the mix that suits you, and that helps every week to get an episode out going to try to make a complete blog post, but sometimes time just doesn't allow it. Brief bullet points would suffice in that situation.

The Min-Time, Max-The Value

This is for those who have little time and would like to make it as simple as humanly possible to do podcasting. There is nothing wrong in the least about that. You may argue that every time, sustainable, average quality production beats rarely-released high-quality audio. After all, the audience wants something normal to hold on to. The solution here is:

1. Format: fly alone.

Present your experience, with faith and panache, on your own, talking mostly on the fly. This suggests very little coordination and eliminates preparation and editing.

2. Facilities: Plain!

Get a good headset mic for yourself, plug it in, and record. Nothing more is required, and the setup time is reduced.

3. Editing: Let it stand out.

Keep it clear and raw. No editing, errors laid bare, and all the more, people will trust and love you.

Publishing: Very appropriate.

Simple notes for the show, just enough to summarize the subject and guide listeners to any resources mentioned.

The Method Balanced

This technique is for those who want to create a display of high quality that represents their brand, but also need to find a dedication to time that makes it sustainable.

1. Format: Co-Hosted, or Interview, respectively.

Bring a co-host with you, or do interviews. Both raise variety, and the latter shares the interviewing and editing jobs.

2. Equipment: An easy setup for a pro. Buy a decent in-person digital recorder, pro mics and records. Or, for remote recording, two decent headset mics.

3. Editing: The approach to click
 Add the title music and outro, and use the Click approach to edit just the major mistakes.
4. Publishing: Post to blog
Produce a blog post of 400 words covering the show's key points and linking to related tools.

The Polished Producer
Using the polished producer approach for those for whom only the best will do. It can take anytime from some days to several weeks for a show to be made, so investing is only for those with a lot of time and resources.
Format: Documentary Style

Working with 1 or 2 speakers and interviews with different individuals, weaving all material into a narrative

1. Instruments: Full shebang

Working in the studio with pro microphones and mixers, plus the field set-up for the pro interview.

3. Editing: Master generating audio

You edit sentence by sentence to construct a show like this. This is time consuming. A great deal of time.

4. Publishing: Article of the Pillar

You would like to construct an article of equal quality to complement a display of this calibre. Spend time on the subject with an article on the 800+ word pillar.

5. Launching and promoting

Have several episodes already finished and uploaded to create hype on launch day via email and social media, disclose the launch in advance to your business network. Before you start, you want to create an audience. Encourage new listeners to sign up to your podcast and leave comments to increase your chances of being heard and eventually featured by iTunes.

Come up with ways you can repurpose your podcast material on your blog and social media platforms to get the best out of your podcast. As well, be accessible and ready to learn about the needs of your listeners through how they react to your content. If your listeners are current or future clients, this is extremely relevant.

6. Artwork

The trick to getting individuals interested in your podcast is great cover art. Alongside your podcast feed, your podcast artwork will appear, as well as (by default) any podcast that the listener downloads to their smartphone.

This is both a marketing tool and something that people can see each week (or upload as much as you do), so you want it to look nice and show all that your podcast stands for.

Although opting for something creative is great, several podcasts prefer to include the name in the artwork centrally.

It is helpful in identifying it in apps that sort your podcasts by tiles, specifically when you need to scroll through a lot of podcasts. Make sure it's bright and fill the frame either way, as people can see it as both a tiny thumbnail and an 'album art' that fills the entire screen of their phone.

Some podcatchers also allow the use of a different picture for each individual podcast episode. Although some podcasts stick to the same image, others use this as an excuse to use a thematic image, such as a still from the TV episode that they are reviewing, or a special piece of artwork based on the episode.

It is not really necessary (and could be a copyright legal issue), but it is something to recommend working forward.

5. STORYTELLING: COMMUNICATION SECRETS BEHIND PROFITABLE AUDIO STORYTELLING AND HOW TO GIVE VALUE TO YOUR AUDIENCE

In action, nuance, and description, storytelling has changed over time, but what has remained stoically intact, either by design or default, is that it remains the viewer's story and their humanity. As story subjects and campaign ambassadors, Richard Ambani and his co-stars became storytellers themselves, creating their own community and helping fuel social change. FilmAid was able to link its story with its most critical viewer by co-creating with its intended audience and gaining their trust, involvement and support in reducing violence.

As the video comes to an end and the credits scroll across the screen, there is pin-drop silence. The melodious buzz that occurs is easily nipped in the bud by the coordinator of the post-screening debate, whose presence calms the audience.

The film's intended audience was predominantly unemployed young people, who were previously known as the key abusers. The producers of the film cast much of the film with young people from this target audience with the goal of making the film hit this demography. Richard Ambani, a community member, was cast by FilmAid as Morio, the main protagonist, who took a journey of self-discovery and changed from an offender into a female champion. We have to make our tales intrinsically interact with the viewer if we want audiences to move beyond just passive customers of our art. Healthy narratives are reflections of society's hearts, in which we can find ourselves and disclose our faults.

Richard recovered his spirit and morality like his role by becoming a central contributor to his audience's social transition. Podcasting, which started about a decade ago, freed radio from timetable tyranny and turned the famously fleeting audio medium into a flourishing ecosystem. Cheap digital recorders and open editing tools such as Hindenburg have made it simpler than ever before to produce audio stories, ranging from expanded journalism and investigative journalism to deeply personal stories and the treatment of ideas and problems in poetic or impressionistic terms.

Recognizing the audience begins with the basis of a great story. That's because in fundraising or communication materials, when we share tales, we don't just tell a story for the sake of telling a tale. To attain a certain purpose, we are telling a lie. For example, the idea is that using a narrative is a strategic move and you want to utilize the story. The goal could be to raise a certain sum of money. To do so, you have to know who you are relating that story to. The truth is, knowing who you're talking to is one of the biggest element affecting the success of your company in telling stories, fundraising, and communications.

Fundraisers and orators, often time again, ask me how they can get to know their audience better and what to do with that data. There are a few tips for this cycle, as well as a resource that will help you hone in on your audience (at the bottom of the post). As a charitable space speechwriter, I had the chance to collaborate with some of the most talented people on the planet. They can quote change theories and apply mathematical tools to just about any problem. But ask them to tell you a story, and they're freezing. You know they can tell a good story. You saw them in the restaurant at lunch or dinner or swapped stories.

There is just something about the "tell me a story" trigger that makes people worry about the constraints rather than the opportunities. Should I have said that? Are people going to care? What if I don't know how it ends and what if the way we wished wouldn't end? Consequently, what often comes out is a formulaic story rather than a genuine moment, which are the kinds of stories that we can aspire to tell. Going outside the comfort zones to tell stories that matter, we can break away from the storytelling rut in our organisation.

The organisation should start telling multiple stories today: Stories with an "I." It's a frequent thing I hear from people employed in the non-profit sector: "I'm not the story." Nevertheless, storytelling is almost always more effective in the first person than in the third. First-person tales are more likely to reveal flaws and show credibility, catch and engage with viewers. Encourage your peers to begin with "I" as subjects that have been influenced by their encounters to speak about themselves. But that doesn't mean that our supporters should be overlooked.

Instead, allow them to share their own tales, rather than making them told second-hand by your organization. Failure

Tales. Many of the fables we were taught as infants had happy endings and our first entrance way to storytelling. But not all of it we try in the field of social change is an immediate success. We ultimately struggle if we take chances (and we should), which can yield some of the most useful stories of education, assessing and changing direction, all of which are essential to accelerating effects.

If your company is still a threat, remind them that any loss, whether it's a revelation or a transition, has its own happy ending. A tale without a happy ending, honestly, is one whose end has not arrived. In marketing, storytelling has a simple and important value—and no, it's not only intended to string consumers along with some fantasy. Storytelling helps elucidate the history and, most importantly, the meaning of your brand. Today, consumers have a vast range of options, and when factors like cost and quality are comparable, customers judge brands more than any other criterion by their intent.

They want to purchase from a business that they feel great at helping. It turns out that aim is also important for workers. A Deloitte study found that over 80percent of the total of workers working for a purpose-driven business believed their company would expand in the coming year. They also are more likely to agree that the highest priority was their customers and less likely to believe that financial benefit was the primary goal. When the Origin market research community set out to measure the storytelling edge, some unexpected results were found. Paintings with the personal tale of an artist increased by 11 % in quality, while 2 otherwise similar eBay listings controlled very different values.

The article with a short fictional work connected to the brand received bids that were 64 % higher. While businesses are being fined left and right for making unfounded statements and misleading consumers with their ads, there are still those who know the importance of putting true stories first and foremost. For example, Airbnb dedicates a whole section of its website to telling stories of customers. Without clients, Airbnb and many other enterprises will have no business both inside and outside the shared economy.

Storytelling, particularly despite the highly busy market, is an important component of the marketing campaign of any product. Focus on these three tactics to help bring in the audience: Sometimes, we assume a lot about who our audience is. We think, mostly, that they're like us and that's not always the reality. I also often see organisations describing their audience too narrowly (by suggesting that their audience is "donos"), which is often not helpful. To get to know your real audience, it is essential to go through a process of exploration.

How're you doing this? You can begin with the information that you have in your database from things like past audience surveys, Google Analytics, and data. Between various pieces like this, you can draw several inferences about your audience. But at some stage, you will need to speak to people. Make a phone call for others. Have a couple of discussions with main stakeholders. Where the jewels are, are in these one-on-one conversations. You will learn about how self-identify your constituents, what complex terminology they use to speak about the cause and (most significantly) why they like your organization's work.

There needs to be a dynamic arc, similar to when you say a novel. Your story has an endpoint, or a conclusion, that goes with fiction or a historical piece, too. Anything else, listeners are lost. Note, your words can't be understood, so you must never believe that. For instance, if the podcasters are addressing a current topic or an interview, they need to understand what they want to get out of the conversation. What aspects of the story are you trying to reveal? What is it that the viewer needs to know? Think about what you want to reveal in your story. Those who enjoy watching movies or reading books know that there still needs to be a tension and a storyline in a good story.

"These two components are what create a decent presentation of a roller coaster ride that keeps subscribers at the edge of their seats, asking "What's next?" There are many devices that can improve your story's level of suspense. As it is done here in this tale of a woman who was born without fibula bones and grew up to be a successful runner, actor and designer, one way is to relate a story sequentially and build up to a climactic end. Another way is to plop the listener right in the middle of the action and then go backwards in time to show how all this happened.

Zak Ibrahim's story, which starts with the discovery that his father was involved in the bombing of the World Trade Centre, is a great example of this. He then travels back to tell his childhood events and how he grew up to take an opposite path than his father's. We've already spoken about how older material on your website does not get the exposure you want. Luckily, it's easy to learn how to get visitors to your page from your past posts, not just the new shiny ones. You'll want to review some of your existing content to do this. This lets you prolong your best posts' lifetime.

Plus, it's perfect for the Search Engine Optimization (SEO) of your website, as 'fresh' and interesting content appears to get a boost. So take a look at your archives, and find articles that can benefit from a makeover. You may need to update old references and links or take any chances after the initial publication into account. The most critical aspect that users and search engines look for is high quality content. A quality piece of content is typically a detailed report about a particular subject that covers all the information for a website. It is also wise to produce 'evergreen' content, i.e., articles that will stay just as valid despite the time. For consumers, this makes it incredibly useful.

Such systematic papers are referred to as 'pillar articles.' They can be referred to as flagship articles or cornerstone articles by other professionals. These are essentially the most valuable articles. In one long-form article, you need to pick the most successful term and then include as many details as possible. To cover all the relevant keywords in your field, you can build as many pillar articles as possible. Timing is difficult to understand. We also thrive on the views around us when it comes to telling a story. "Are they getting it?" and "Are they enjoying it?" and most obviously: "Should I change the topic because the listeners are getting bored?"

The question is not if you can change the subject or not, or whether they agree, it's whether audiences are still enthralled. Every subject has a deadline, and we tune out at some level. We won't even listen to an hour-long story about a dog on a stroll, for instance. Yet, we can listen to an hour-long story about a dog that saved the police force's lots of lives. We should accept that one story is more powerful and could probably maintain our concentration all the way through.

Video captures viewers informs that other media clearly do not. There is a human propensity to commiserate with what we see in others, making a video an incredibly efficient way to elicit the viewer's emotions. "Whether it's your Chief executive giving a view of the organization, a product demonstration video with screenshots, an illustrated smart board video breaking down complex subject matter or a personal testimony from one of your customers, a video gets everyone on the same track, and use the same story and the right messaging. Whether it's your CEO giving an overview of the business, a product demonstration video with screenshots, an animated whiteboard video breaking down complicated topic matter or a personal testimony from one of your clients, more than half of the worldwide business analysts polled report video has the highest ROI of all their different topics.

Video is the ideal tool for highlighting the intent of your brand from a marketing perspective. Why was the firm founded? What influence do you plan to have on your customers and the world? Your viewer has an interest for tales, and film will convey yours to your audience genuinely in a process that encourages them to make a purchase. In reality, research has found out that after seeing a branded social video, as many as 64 percent of viewers will purchase a product. It's certainly unrealistic, but if you want to get the most out of your branded content, you'll need to make it a little less "branded."

To create a great narrative and then water down its influence by throwing a huge logo in the centre of it is not rare for brands. Classically, they are drawn to legitimacy and occasionally encounter this. Try to avoid overtly creating a narrative about your brand. Instead, concentrate on creating a good story and organically let the word get out. To get a group's interest, assess the impact of yelling to talking quietly and forcing them to listen. Storytelling is a vital part of a marketing strategy, but it's not just a yarn that you should spin.

It is important to create compelling content for both electronic and in-person consumption, and that sometimes means making your brand take a back seat to the larger story. Although the upswing in your marketing ROI is most likely to be noticed, your audience will note your focus on excellent and genuine content. To deliver a successful Google-friendly PowerPoint presentations, you can use a platform such as SlideShare, thus increasing your visibility. If you do it well, you can drive a high amount of traffic for free, and your presentations get famous, which they can get on this website easily, and the presentation links to your website.

For audio storytelling, I'm far from great. Yet, I've experienced more in ten weeks than I ever thought I could. Time, preparation, and discipline are required. It's an experience, actually, and it's enjoyable. Everybody loves to chat. Audio storytelling has no limits. Your speech, with or without a screen to back it up, is a powerful weapon. It has the ability to attract attention, share awareness, tell stories, paint the picture, re-enact history, and give you perspectives into someone's life without any images. Similar to a climax, an S.T.A.R. moment is an experience that is so dramatic that your audience can talk about it weeks later. "Something they will always remember."

This can come in the form of dramatization, offensive images, or startling statistics, according to presentation expert Nancy Duarte in her book Resonate. In a 2009 TED talk, Bill Gates referred to this tactic when he made the argument for growing investment in malaria eradication. "He gave statistics to demonstrate how serious the issue was and then stunned the room by opening a bottle full of mosquitoes, saying, "There is no excuse why only poor people should have the experience. When you think outside of the box, this is the move. "If this were me, what would they ask?" If this were me, what would they ask?

Learn the significance of your story and what your audience are trying to tell you. Within the conversation itself, this is how you develop. If they are clear about their perception of their ultimate result, you're clear about what questions need to be answered. When it comes to your equipment, planning is also crucial. Be sure to have your microphone and recorder if you're doing an interview outside the studio, or even if you're capturing natural sound. Once you've done some discovery and have accumulated enough data points, you're going to start seeing some patterns in your audience. You are going to find that not everyone is alike, but they have similar data points.

What you want to concentrate on are those popular data points. These are the facts about the target group that will be helpful when making strategic choices about fundraising and communication materials. What's even more helpful with this knowledge is to build an audience profile. A mock-up of a fictitious audience member is the audience persona. You provide them with a title, image, story of life, demographic information (from your research), etc. The purpose of making this composite is to have a very clear image of who you're talking to. For a free worksheet that you can access and use to create your audience profile, scroll to the bottom of the page!

You can use a website such as SlideShare to offer powerful Google-friendly PowerPoint presentations, effectively raising your visibility. If you do this right, you can move a massive amount of traffic for free, and your presentations go viral, which they can easily use on this website, and the presentation links to your website. Do not forget that audio transmits non-verbal meaning, which can be just as relevant as words: do not edit a pause, a gulp, a breath. Listen to this reporter from Australia explain how she comforted a dying American soldier in Vietnam who'd been blown up by a mine.

I tried both formats by incorporating her overwhelming feelings and gulping delivery to express the terror of war even more effectively than the same words expressed on the page. "As UK broadcaster Seán Street puts it, audio creates the best images, sound is subjective, "a collaboration between memory and imagination. Instead of being the passive recipient of pictures on TV, an audio narration invites each audience to co-create the story. PRODUCTION: log the audio, analyse the content and mention its usability (rather than transcribe) (great quality sound, pithy etc.) Use conversational, not formal, language- is English, use contractions,' we're',' will not' etc. when drafting your study. Try filming on-the-spot spontaneous narration, explaining what you see. If it malfunctions, you can still dump it, but it adds urgency when it works.

Grow your audience: how to get traffic (free and paid methods)

A lot of people think that SEO can be a perfect way for a website to generate traffic. For most of us, however, search engine optimization could be our only way to improve search results and increase traffic. This can be a horrible thing. It is critical that you know how to expand the traffic that comes to your website and not rely solely on the optimization of search engines. Alternatively, if your primary source of traffic fails, it might mean the end of your business. In this article, we're going to take a look at how you can improve traffic on websites and blog posts without relying solely on SEO.

We'll look at a range of tactics you can put in place right now and how you can maximize each traffic source. By the end of this book, you would have the peace of mind you need to know that your site is not going to crash and burn, only because of a shift in the algorithm of Google. Let's start! Publishing a blog post on your website or translating an interview with an industry influencer into a blog post will help to drive traffic both through organic search and through the influencer who promotes the content to their public (see the backlinks section above).

This can also help add so much wide range to your content and show that you are active in your field to your visitors. Conversely, in their own review or round-up post, you could ask the influencer to mention your business. This technique is still free, but you still need to collaborate with the influencer to be an exchange with mutual advantage. You can also be a guest blogger. In your neighbourhood, identify complementary companies whose audience is relevant to your company. See if you can contribute a post with a link back to your website to their blog. Make sure that your content is relevant to their audience and helpful so that it is more of an even exchange.

If you hope that more traffic to your site will also result in more sales, as part of your paid search strategies, you will need to target significant economic intent keywords.

Yeah, it can be competitive (and expensive) to fight for these search keywords, but the payoffs can be worth it. That's not enough to create quality content and hope that the people find it, you have to be strategic. To promote your content, one of the best ways to improve traffic to your website is to use social media platforms. For fast, snappy (and tempting) links, Twitter is perfect, while Google+ promotion will help your site appear in customized search results and appears to be particularly successful in B2B niches. If you're a B2C product company, with image-heavy social sites such as Pinterest and Instagram, you could find great traction. More guidance on making the most of social media marketing is available here.

You run the risk of being blocked from online advertisement sites or, even worse, being banned from Google if your website receives bot traffic. It's not worth the cheap website traffic! Take the time to develop your site with stable and consistent traffic. As described above, if those visitors are not likely to connect with your sites, turn into leads, or become customers, there is no point in bringing more traffic to your website. It does not change quickly to boost the website traffic. It requires work, but the effort you put in is going to be equal to the value of the traffic you make.

Plus, we have excluded the hardest part for you: understanding what to do in the first place. You can get the right visitors to your website by using Google My Company and the other secure channels mentioned above. More importantly, more of those visitors turn into customers. So many companies concentrate on attracting new customers through content marketing that they forget about more conventional methods. Email marketing can be a powerful method, and even a mildly effective email blast can lead to a substantial traffic increase. Just be careful not to flood people in your company with relentless emails for every single update.

Also, don't ignore the power of word-of-mouth advertising, particularly from individuals who already enjoy your goods or services. A friendly reminder with an email about a new service or item can also help you increase your traffic. First of all, a disclaimer-do not spam Reddit and other similar sites in the hope of referral traffic "hitting the jackpot," because it will not happen. Communities like Reddit are extraordinarily knowledgeable about spam disguised as legitimate links, but it does not hurt to submit links every now and again that these audiences will find truly useful.

Choose a subreddit, send your content, then watch the traffic pour in. Traffic to your website helps increase your rating, which creates more traffic, but you want to make sure that the traffic increase is also related to an increase in engagement. You don't bring in the right traffic if your traffic increases, but your conversion rates decrease. There are a various ways to utilize your site for converters, in the correct locations, and including declarations and lead capture types, giving instructions your visitors are looking for, and making navigation simple and efficient.

But the very first process is to bring the best visitors to your site in the first place. Your objective is to drive more qualified visitors to your site when it comes to website traffic. That is, those who are most likely to turn into leads and clients. There are two ways that you can effectively drive traffic to the site. It's free the first way. It includes things like optimization of the search engine, setting up a blog, marketing social media, and so on and so on. Another way is to pay. Everybody knows that paid advertising can drive traffic to a website, but it can be expensive as well.

If you don't comprehend stuff like conversion rates and click monitoring to see how much a transaction costs you, then you'll definitely struggle with paid traffic. There are some fantastic ways to drive traffic to your website that fall into all of these areas, whichever way you slice it. But, the more structured you are, the more you've introduced your deal at the outset, the more likely you're going to be to drive traffic to your website. So, how do you monitor all of your efforts to ensure that when it comes to driving traffic to your website, you do the best to comprehend where your visitors are coming from?

Using Google Analytics is the most rudimentary and straightforward way. And I'm not just talking about Google Analytics being installed. . In fact, if you're not too tech knowledgeable, Google has a great tool that you can use to build your URLs. The tool can be found here. Two fields, 1) the URL itself, and 2) the campaign's source, are required.

The source of the campaign can be anything like email or cost-per-click or any other source you use to place advertisements and drive traffic. Here, you can also add the name of the campaign, Like a Facebook deal or a summer sale or a new line of goods or something else. Be sure to separate the underscoring spaces. This way, you know where that traffic comes from when you drive traffic. Otherwise, in the dark, you are left.

For instance, if you do some content marketing on Quora.com or Medium.com, you could use the source of the campaign simply as Quora or Medium and the medium of the campaign as content marketing and the term as the term for which you are working. Get this image? Then, in Google Analytics, you will see all the beautiful results directly, and you will know specifically where your traffic comes from. All right, so this gives you a sense of the general areas from which your traffic comes and how your traffic can be monitored. Remember, you are wasting your time marketing online if you're not tracking the traffic that's coming to your website.

You need to comprehend where it comes from when you drive traffic to any website, blog or wherever, to encourage you to scale up your efforts. The other important thing about monitoring is the use of conversion pixels to be able to accurately assess explicitly down to the cent, how much each sale costs you. For instance, if you spent $100 on Facebook ads, resulting in 200 clicks, without knowing exactly you just lost $100 on how many of those clicks resulted in a transaction. Let's just say that you received 3 sales out of the 200 clicks, which were tracked with a conversion pixel from Facebook. Those 3 sales resulted in revenue of $800.

Now, and while it may sound obvious, when trying to drive traffic to your website, it can be easily overlooked. High traffic statistics can be a wonderful thing, but the figures are only vanity indicators if the traffic is not driven. As we discuss the subject of growing traffic to your site, this is something to bear in mind. One thousand untargeted visits are not the same as 100 targeted visits. A social media network might generate web traffic, but your website might not be of high quality.

Yotpo collected data from 65 million e-retail orders representing 2 billion dollars in sales value from 120,000 e-Commerce merchants to determine the most significant web traffic sources for eCommerce websites. So far, we have only talked about improvements you can make to your current website and blog. However, if you choose to learn how to get traffic to the site, you'll want to consider increasing what's offered. You can consider adding a forum and/or a knowledge base to your website, just to name two examples.

A forum can be particularly effective in boosting traffic because it allows individuals to do more than just consume content passively.Building a community around your website is a perfect way to keep people coming back. As for knowledge bases, they let you answer your audience's most critical questions and provide a vehicle for self-help. Publishing succinct 'Q&A' articles can also help you get featured in the 'response boxes' of Google—another big traffic engine.

6. HOW DO YOU PICK GUESTS FOR YOUR PODCAST AND HANDLE THEM

There are several advantages of running an interview series, as well as downsides. One of those downsides is facing the difficulty of always trying to select guests for the podcast.

Eventually, when it comes to finding the right guests for your show, and your audience, this give you a few avenues to explore.

The initial step should always be your content when selecting possible podcast guests. What benefit is this individual going to add to your audience? What unique perspectives are you going to gain from them?

Where are you starting? Where do you look? How do you understand who to approach? And how do you go about keeping them in touch?

Market yourself and your show: with podcasting, a good deal of marketing is involved. Your invitation for an interview allows the potential interviewee to sell your services. If you are part of a network for podcasting, be sure to note that. It is often beneficial to have high listenership numbers. Have you ever done interviews? Do any name dropping, if so.

And if it is, with other podcasters, a good place to begin could be. They want to get their names out and their audience to expand as well.

Be versatile: you're asking for their time, mind. Your timetable and theirs can have limitations. Often, within 24 hours, you will get an interview or you have to arrange it weeks or months in advance. You can have to take time off work or reorganize other plans from your daily job.

Prepare double the amount of questions you feel you're going to need. For no reason other than the interviewer believed the guest would talk his head off on the first question, some interviews you hear come to a halt.

Jot down a series of questions with short, one-or-two-word responses that could fill your podcast.

This manner, you have a secret collection of questions to call upon if you find yourself struggling. After a few short replies, you can still fall back on "Would you please elaborate on that a bit?"

Don't ever worry about a dumb question being posed. Remember when answering questions that might sound obvious or commonly asked: It is possible that your audience has never heard them answered before. All right, maybe a writer has been asked over and over again, "Where are your ideas coming from?" Or the politician heard, "So, when did you enter politics first? Often.

Meeting guests on their own grounds

Be calm, be relaxed, and be good. When taking your podcast on the road, these same rules apply. You may find yourself in the home, place of business, or some other neutral place of a person. For lack of a better word, you are now practicing tactical journalism, attacking innocent individuals with questions that may not strike you as intense and probing, but may be for individuals who do not anticipate them. Wherever you are when the interview is conducted, make sure to show respect to your guests.

A better tactic to having good interviews is to ask your visitors for permission to interview them, be they passers-by or experts at their place of business.

It is hardly a perfect way to introduce yourself and your podcast to the world by shoving a microphone in someone's face and spewing out questions. If there is a handler or representative for the guest you want to interview, it is good protocol to obey the recommendations and advice of the guest's staff.

Most people open up and are happy to chat if you start with a soft, inviting smile and clarify what you're doing and why.

Getting started with your niche

Firstly, are there other podcasts that cover the same subject as you? Are any of them doing interviews? If so, take a look and listen to see if you and your audience will be a good match for any of these guests.

If anyone has already accepted to be a podcast guest, then there is a fair chance that they will be able to do the same again. In addition, podcasts that operate for a longer time offer a greater chance of ranking for a search result compared to a short one. Before awarding you the precious top spots, search engines are still searching for trust in your posts from the audience. Some subjects are very competitive, such as wellness, personal finance, fitness, culinary, weight loss, etc., and it could take some time to catch the audience's attention, it may be several months before you get ranked in a pretty good position to have any significant audience.

Look for Bloggers & YouTubers

Be mindful not to replicate the same interview your preferred guest has done elsewhere while moving down this path. Learn how to approach your questions from a different perspective, even though you're after the same stories and main takeaways. For yourself, your guest, and your listeners, this will keep things exciting and enjoyable. Who creates content in blog form on your topic (or a related one) or on YouTube? If anyone wanted to chat about the same stuff as you, there's a fair chance that they'd be more than glad to come to your show.

This can not only provide useful, meaningful content for you, it can also help improve your viewer numbers. Your respondent, who might be involved in your other shows, will definitely share the episode with their very own group or community. A variety of your listeners may also see the respondent checking out their blog or clips. Everyone on here wins.

Traditional media

There are individuals that are important to your subject on TV, radio, newspapers, or magazines. And you'd be shocked by how many of them would be pleased and able to have a talk on your podcast if you approached them.

There are typically a variety of ventures on the go for reporters, authors, and folks working in the industry. Their company is all about getting to an audience. Why don't they want to communicate with you?

Find someone who sells stuffs

Lately, if anyone has written a book relevant to your topic they would likely jump at the opportunity to come to your podcast and communicate to your listeners about it. Your audience is their intended audience as well.

Make sure that you create an informative interview that is significant and useful to your listeners, as with any product sales guest. They shouldn't have to go ahead and buy a commodity for the interviewee. Avoid one big sales pitch becoming the entire discussion. Not only can this wreck an episode, but in fact, put a black spot on your podcast.

It may be helpful to clarify beforehand to the interviewee that you're going to talk about a variety of points. Let them understand that you'll ask them about their product at the end of the conversation. This is where you are going to give them an opportunity to chat about it. Then, indicate where people will go to purchase it.

This also helps to weed out the more general requests received by podcasters. To locate shows to survey their customers, some lazy PR companies prefer to use a scatter-gun system.

You may also look at setting up an affiliate link or code. You have the chance, this way, to receive a commission on any products sold. However, the major issue, by far, is making quality content.

Ask other guests from the Podcast

When you are done with interview, ask if they know anyone else who would be a good choice to come to the show. After the interview is done, you should do this immediately. Or, you can do it by email later on, perhaps when you tell them that their episode is live. I guess the easiest thing is to do it when you're already on the phone with them.

You've just spent considerable time talking this way, and you'll get an instant response. You have the additional credibility of referencing the interviewee who thought of them as you approach other potential podcast guests. 'I recently talked to [this guest] on my podcast. He did suggest that I contact you to see if you would like to come to the exhibition too'.

You've developed some common interests instantly, and most audiences will be very open to it. If the talk went very well with your initial guest, you might get a direct access to their contact.

Just ask the listeners

Inquire with your audience about Potential podcast guests that they would like to hear on the show will recommend your listeners. Some may be fantastic future guests themselves, potentially. Encourage individuals to get in contact with you. At the end of each episode, include it in your call to action.

Often, make it simple for individuals to get in contact with you. Sending anyone to a page like your website.com/contact is a good idea, where people can choose their favourite way of dropping you a line.

To send a request to appear on your podcast, you can also create a form exclusively for potential interviewees.

Getting in contact with future guests for the podcast

Social networking can be a simple and convenient way for future podcast guests to reach out. But I often think the most powerful approach here is email.

The primary thing is to be conscious of people's time and, though always in a friendly manner, get to the point quickly with your request. Imagine that your prospective interviewee checks their phone and spots your Eight hundred words email while walking down the street. Do you think they are going to read it fully?

Here is a simple format that you may want to adopt

Hello [name], how are you doing?

I'm [name] from [podcast] and I would love to get you to talk about [specific topic] sometime on the program. I think the [interest in the subject] will be very good for our audience.

(Alternatively, let them know where you discovered them or from where you know them. "I read your story recently, and

I really loved it" or "I just saw your [topic] video, and..." that sort of stuff.)

Here is my calendar connection if you are up for it, you can book a slot which works for you.

For this method, getting a calendar connection or booking tool is indispensable. There are plenty of choices. A service like this cuts out all the back and forth that might cause the scanner to drop off a potential interviewee.

Note to have an email signature put in place with a direct connection to the website of your show, too. Any future podcast guests can click through that way, where they can find out who else was on your show. They might also have some of your episodes to listen to.

How to record guests who are remote

Often you may want to document a visitor in the room who is not with you. They could be someone you meet online, someone you've arranged an interview with, or maybe one of your frequent visitors who can't make it in. This is never perfect, but there are several reasonably simple ways to record and compile audio from a distance into a podcast.

Through your VOIP app of choice, such as Skype, Zoom or Google Hangouts, you can speak to each other; voice calls function better, as video can strain bandwidth and reduce audio quality. Although there are many remote recording software options, the simplest (and cheapest) way is simply to record the audio of each person using Audacity or Audition separately.

You will want to begin by counting or clapping together in sync, a process known as 'setting a mark'. You will be able to line up these marks together when you edit the different files together later on, ensuring that your replies to each other sound normal and do not cut through the other respondents.

Many podcasters are fascinated with 'room tone', the notion that when recorded in different rooms, podcasts sound very unique. In order to avoid differences in sound quality, you may want to ensure that the participants record with the same settings (such as mic levels) and the same equipment.

In order to reduce the echo and reverb of larger spaces, hanging up sheets and tactically positioned cushions are DIY remedies.

Approach Important Personalities

Each subject and niche does have its "celebrities". It can also be difficult to meet these people if you're podcasting in such a busy environment. They've possibly delegated reading it to an assistant if anyone is so famous that they get 100+ email messages a day. There is a risk that yours will be seen as "just another invitation for a podcast interview" and discarded without a reply.

If there is anyone you'd really love to have on the show, then maybe you could record audio or video of your message to them. This has a much better chance of going through their filters, practically. It illustrates that you're not just sending out emails of jokey copy and paste. If you are doing it, be professional.

Don't ever take the simplistic approach of solely going after guests because they have a major social media presence. This will, of course, be a great perk. But the scale of their follow-up is not necessarily equal to your episode's extra listeners. Particularly if you don't stand out that much for them to post the interview you are doing with them.

Maintaining the program running and on schedule often includes refined skills in moderation. Your guests will probably be very excited about the topic at hand, which is ideal, but this can also contribute to lengthy monologues, random tangents, and conversation supremacy. You need to be able to direct individuals back on track politely, yet tactfully, which is a delicate, complex ability to master.

It is also an example where you could more efficiently use social media. For instance, in a video you have recorded for them on Instagram, you might tag someone. It relies on your own personal choice, and whether or not you use these sites for your prospective guest.

7. TECHNICAL ASPECTS: HOW TO RECORD A PROFESSIONAL-SOUNDING PODCAST EVEN IF YOU'RE A BEGINNER

What is the App Podcatcher?

A podcatcher is a software application you use to automatically listen to and monitor all the podcast feeds you choose to have downloaded.

Good podcatcher clients usually allow you to monitor when and how often they search for updates and download new shows automatically and place them in the media player of your choosing. Some suggest putting them for your manual intervention on your hard drive.

Podcast Equipment

It is indicated that most individuals do not go into podcasting to collect tons of fancy and costly audio equipment. Of course, some folks do end up doing it, but you certainly don't need to.

Instead of whether or not your long chain of gear is all working properly, it is easier to start basic so that you can concentrate on your real material. With time, you can tweak and upgrade stuff in between and as you evolve.

When you're just starting out, podcast recording equipment can be frustrating to rummage through and pick. You can get a lot of podcast equipment, but that doesn't mean you have to have it all, and you can still extend your podcast equipment list over time.

Features of the Podcast

Many of today's podcatcher clients use the same kind of base source code.

Active directory

This is where it's able to meet clients. It will include all the folders for podcasting and make several lists accessible inside the clients. The majority of podcatchers actually look at just a limited number of the actual available folders. With certain directories being commercially driven by podcatcher clients, it is crucial for listeners to be able to evaluate impartial directory templates, not to indicate that this is happening, but the possibility exists.

Windows Media Support

Windows Media Player is supported by many of the podcatcher clients, but you'll have to do a small volume of work to handle what is uploaded to your media player. This process needs enhancement. Current Windows Media Player-supported podcatcher clients connect shows and files only to the player library, and you also need to pick what will be imported to your media device. When more MP3 players supported by Windows Media Player hit the market, developers would need to pay a little bit more notice to the interface of Windows Media Player.

Apple iTunes support

Since Apple iTunes supports Apple iPods with large capacity, podcatcher support for this media player is almost standard. Integration and synchronization between the two media players is the simplest on Apple iTunes with the customers adding podcasts to the playlist.

BitTorrent features

There is some confusion for general users about how BitTorrent operates and the players who implement it and have the BitTorrent client incorporated in their source code; no additional applications are therefore needed.

Export OPML

You could do the same with family and friends just like people share their list. This function also helps you to back up your subscription list so that you have a simple transfer route if you want to change podcatcher clients in the future.

Displays show notes

While most podcasters publish their podcasts, along with website links to the featured pages, they include a website post with everything discussed in the broadcast. Some podcatcher customers allow you to directly read certain posts in the application.

When podcatcher clients and media players develop, the show notes will advance across the screen of your portable media player as the host talks about each subject, and the related connection will be visible and instantly accessible for the content being discussed.

Free

Most podcatcher clients are free, but some businesses are beginning to build registration-needed podcatcher clients. I am all about upgrades, and I am willing to pay for them, like many of you.

File management capacity: As you strive to keep up with new and creative ways of doing podcasts, you would listen to a large number of podcasts which would make you download a significant number of files every month with all that in mind. These files are handled by some podcatcher clients by tidying up after themselves based on settings you have set in the application's preferences.

Download restriction setups

Whether you're on holiday or on a restricted dial-up link, a time will come when you don't want to download 200 mg of new display data every day from your podcatcher client. Download restriction setups: Whether you're on holiday or on a restricted dial-up link, a time will come when you don't want to download 200 mg of new display data every day from your podcatcher client.

Based on show size and the number of previous shows to download when first subscribing to a show, the best podcatcher clients have features to restrict downloads. You wouldn't want to download two months of old details if you're a new subscriber.

Recording tips for your podcast to get the best sound

When you're producing your own podcast, with great ideas and stories, but starting to work with a small budget, you're probably a writer, journalist, or subject matter expert. Bad audio quality can harm the message you're trying to send, so it's important to have great, convincing audio that sounds great.

You can greatly enhance the sound quality of your podcast with a few easy measures.

Find a comfortable room around you with plenty of space

Whenever you begin to record with a microphone while reading from a script or documenting an interview, think about these things that might make a lot of noise in your environment. On your machine, is there a fan? As you scroll through your script, can you hear button presses?

To track your recordings, use headphones. Before you begin your delivery or interview, turn them up to listen to what the microphone hears. Try to eliminate any extra noise as much as possible. Later in the process, a clearer recording would be simpler to manage.

It's also necessary to think about the sound quality of the room in which you are. As a mirror reflects light, strong, plain surfaces reflect sound. Leave room to eliminate early reflections around you and your microphone. Place yourself on a rug, near some bookcases, and away from the walls. Avoid spaces with reverberation, too. In particular, certain offices, classrooms, meeting rooms, and huddle rooms may be reverberant.

Test with Indirect microphone positioning

Plosives are like massive gusts of wind to a microphone, the blast of air that escapes the mouth as we make "P" and "B" sounds. To help minimize these, stop talking straight into the front of the microphone and, where necessary, use a windscreen or pop filter.

Position the microphone up slightly to the side so that the air bursts do not touch the diaphragm directly. However, don't set it up at too drastic an angle, or in the pickup pattern of directional microphones, you'll talk into a null.

A much more natural tone in your voice should be heard. To see what sounds best for your voice, play with your microphone placement and capture test recordings.

Check the equipment for calling.

If you have scheduled a phone-in (or Skype-in) interview for your podcast with others, such as a favourite singer or politician, plan ahead of time for the interview. To perform a mock interview, Skype (or phone) a friend and ensure that the recording setup not only works, but also sounds fine.

The demand for bandwidth increases the more people you encounter through your device. Reception can be impacted, so if you know that more than one individual is going to be involved in this interview, it's a good idea to test how many individuals in one call can confer effectively.

Get your batteries tested.

If you're using a portable recorder, make sure your batteries are charged and you have spares (such as the Zoom H2). (Also search the spares.) If you're very paranoid or live in an environment with occasional electrical issues, if your main power drops out, you can also pick up an uninterruptable power source.

Check the storage on your hard drive.

Hard drives are becoming larger and less costly, however that doesn't mean that they're unlimited. Audio files can be huge, especially

If you record in a raw format such as WAV or AIFF, you lose time if you run out of room in the middle of recording a show or an interview; you lose track and you lose face with your interviewee in the case of interviews. It's practically the same idea if you're recording on a portable recording unit.

Create a recording of a test

Create a test recording before recording an entire podcast first. Or sit back and listen back to a previous recording and compare it with other podcasts you love. Listen to your test in the setting you want your listeners to be in, from ear plugs to high-fidelity headphones, like a bus, train, or car, and on various listening devices. Take some tips on what could be changed by you. Does your reading trail off at the end of your sentences? Could there be a lot of background noise that you might want to delete, or mouth noise? To get input from trusted colleagues, both on the material and sound quality, you could also use the test recording. You might also send it to one of your top podcast hosts and see if they're going to give you any feedback (and even mention it on one of their podcasts or social media platforms).

Standing and delivering

When recording, several broadcasters and voice-over performers stand to help provide better air support and solid, assured reading. This can also help minimize early reflections induced by a desk. A music stand works well if you need anything to carry your script. To prevent early reflection, consider putting a piece of foam or a carpet sample on the music stand behind your script.

Be conservative about your grades/levels

You will need set an input level for your microphone on most audio interfaces and recorders. There's really no need to set input levels too "hot" with the advent of high-quality digital recording. Later on, you can always make it quieter.

Talk at a normal-to-loud speaking voice and try to make this level about -20 dB, or around halfway up on most meters, to set a nice, modest input level. Then measure to ensure that the level never rises above goes "into the red." with a hearty laugh or emphatic expression. When you're worried that it could, just turn it down and be cautious.

Record a file with high-resolution audio

Compression objects compound over time, so with a high-quality WAV or AIFF file, make your initial recording. However, at any resolution higher than 24 bits, 48 kHz, there is really no need to record a register.

For high-quality source material, even if your recording goes for distribution via a data compression codec (such as MP3 or AAC), it will begin with the finest potential source material.

Working from an outline and taking time to get a perfect delivery

There is no alternative for confident reading and great material, no matter how good your microphone is. With the intrinsic desire to do it live, there are just a few experts.

It's much simpler to edit a script than to edit audio, and it gives you the benefit of getting all your brilliant ideas set out in a text format which could be used for something else, such as a transcript, blog post, or even a book down the line.

Clearly, interview segments and co-host conversation can't be scripted. But with your introductions, questions, transitions, and closings planned, getting a good outline will help create a seamless podcast and show your guests that you have done your homework and are ready and qualified.

It could also be helpful to provide a description of what you're going to talk about up front to your audience, and a review of takeaways at the end. This will set the context for your episode and nicely complete it, which is also a fantastic idea for workshops and pitch meetings.

Record separate remote guests and co-hosts

You should switch to VoIP systems, such as Skype or Google Hangouts, or the telephone while working with visitors and co-hosts who can't be in your studio. The quality of the audio is not always the best, but capturing great audio in both areas is simple and then mixing them together later.

Only ask your remote guest to record only their voice for a high-quality WAV/AIFF file that they can return to you later.

Leave time for revisions

Be sure to leave time for a thorough edit and QC (quality control) of your whole piece while preparing your podcast for recording and deployment. The time of the listener is precious, so make it clear, succinct, and professional with your message. Limit dead air, delete duplicate subjects, and address "umm," "aah" and false starts occasionally.

Even so, editing can be overdone, so push yourself to get the best reading in one section possible. You don't really want to edit the audio to death, but listeners still enjoy brevity!

How a podcast can be recorded

Podcast recording doesn't have to be a complex process. To capture audio from a desk microphone on a laptop or desktop computer, free recording applications such as Audacity can be used.

A Blue Snowball or Blue Yeti USB condenser microphone is used by many podcasters, which offers a specific upgrade to integrated mics at a moderate price, however there are a number of more costly options.

To avoid unwanted feedback, such as coughing or blowing into the mic, you might also want a 'pop filter'. These often cover or sit in front of the microphone (it is the foam cover used on the microphones of Television personalities), often with a flexible arm to tie it to the desk.

They are most effective for outdoor recording, but they are also useful for reducing indoor noise.

Before you hit a record, there are a few settings you can wish to tweak. The number of bytes is an important element in how large the files you make are going to be, and the audio quality after it has been processed.

The Best Tips for Podcast Recording

Great podcast recordings bring it down to the capacity of the host to create the correct sound. Every time you sit down to make an episode, these tips are all about creating the ideal recording atmosphere and actionable strategies you can use.

Using the appropriate services

With your laptop's microphone, you can record a podcast, but we do not suggest it. To record accurate and clear audio, you'll need a few pieces of podcast equipment. This is the simplest of all our tips for podcast recording and it has the greatest effect on the quality of your audio.

Don't forget to warm yourself up

To point out the obvious, it takes a bit of talking to record a podcast show. Instead of going into your session cold, warm your mouth and vocal cords by practicing your script or saying a few tongue twisters, warming up properly will strengthen your dictation and prevent you from stumbling over words. There is nothing more than flawlessly delivering the points the first time around.

Recording in a calm, small room

To minimize outside noise and echoes, record episodes in the smallest and quietest room possible. Shut down your windows and doors, turn off any constant noisy machines or gadgets, and position your pets somewhere they're not going to bother you for a good few hours. With soft objects (couches, pillows, carpet, etc.) that absorb sound to suppress any errant noises, fill your recording area.

It's not enough to have the right microphone. You just have to know how to use it. Watch our video demonstration for the Podcast like a Professional on how to achieve the ideal mic technique!

Watch the rate of volume

You can monitor the volume levels as you record, as you keep the microphone distance constant. Most recording software shows levels from green, yellow, to red as a scale.

For your usual conversational tone and yellow parts, keep your volume in the green section when you need to add emphasis. Keep out of the red section or there will be distortions in your voice.

Creating a brief profile for noise

At the beginning of your recording, pause for four or five seconds to generate a noise profile. Keep completely quiet and remove all noise from the environment. During editing, you can use this moment of silence to recognize and eliminate any background noise by using Audacity when eliminating noise.

Implement proper strategies for microphones

First, at the same height as your mouth, put your microphone. Then lay quietly a couple of inches and have the pop filter between the mic and your mouth. First, concentrate on the distance of your mouth from the configuration of the microphone and adapt your body to the amount of volume needed. Note, the closer you are to your microphone, the better your voice sounds.

While you can adjust the volume level of your voice during post-production to maintain it consistent, by holding your mouth the same distance from the mic while recording, reduce your editing time.

Look at your breathing.

We all just need to breathe, so it will stop any major gusts of wind from creeping into your recording by monitoring the sound of your inhales and exhales. Sit upright, consider taking smaller breaths for a louder inhalation, or switch your mouth away from the microphone entirely when you need to take a large breath.

Always hold your body still

When filming, moving the body around causes background noise. This happens a lot if you use headphones with ear buds. The wire lies close to your chest, which causes your shirt and neck to brush against the microphone. Try to sit still with your feet planted in your chair. Stop shifting stuff on your desk around. If you write your ideas on paper, also pass them around as quietly as you can.

Early solving of sound problems

Before officially starting to dive into your episode, make a test recording. If your guest's microphone is a concern or you can hear building crew outside, don't try to push through. From the beginning, recognize and address audio problems or even wait to record.

The worst case scenario is to record a complete episode only to discover that in editing there is a bigger problem you can't solve.

Although a podcast episode can be recorded without headphones, you'll probably get a lot of audio feedback. Have everybody wear headphones to clean it up, so you don't have to waste precious editing hours.

Keep silent when talking to your guests

While your guests talks, it's tempting to drop into simple sentences such as "yes" and "true" and "alright. These are natural parts of language that we use without knowing, however your listeners may be disturbed by them. Well, during editing, you can delete them, but that is a lot of unnecessary work. Training yourself to restrict interjections is simpler and helps the guest or co-host to finish their thinking.

Leave audio labels for errors

Errors happen. In your episode, they're not trapped forever because you're not performing live. It's simple podcast editing to cut out errors, but you need to give yourself a hint to find them on the list.

There have been, thankfully, a few ways to do this. You can insert a spoken marker where you say "delete the pizza restaurant story." Then take a pause for a few seconds and keep going. Seek those delays during editing, and delete the errors. Another selection is a high-pitch sound marker that will create a boost in the volume level, like a dog clicker. After the error happens, press it a few times and then find the spikes while editing.

Mute when you're not talking

When your co-host or guest talks, save yourself some editing work by muting your microphone. You're not going to pick up their speech on your microphone this way, and it's less noise that you're going to have to delete later.

Using elements of output sparingly

The effects of sound have their place. To your show, they will add life and individuality. But they can also interrupt them too much and use them cheaply. Where the content calls for it, use sound effects only and adhere to effects that fit the brand.

Remain hydrated

Try to drink seven ounces of water before the recording takes place. This is going to relax the stomach, open the jaw, and help the concentration. As our mouths dry, it will also decrease any mouth clicks, the natural clicking and popping noises we create.

Our position is that drinking more water and pausing to use the toilet once or twice is safer than suffering from the symptoms of dehydration.

Report under a blanket

A simple way to minimize background noise if you're trapped in a noisy environment is to cover a blanket over you and your microphone. This technique is crude, but it works. This is helpful if you're forced to document your car or apartment building in a busy hotel.

Do not be afraid to take a break for a moment.

Try to split the show into groups of logical locations to take a break for you. For any problems, it's great to double check the audio, catch more water, and stretch to stay loose for your whole recording session.

Breaks are also good times for your co-host or guest to explore what's next. You can schedule your chat, review notes, and even rehearse your conversation.

Maximize the bandwidth on the Internet

It is so essential that you improve your communication as much as possible if you are having an interview or discussion over the internet. This will enhance the audio quality that your recording program records.

How are you boosting your bandwidth?

Well, all you can do is plug directly into your router (instead of connecting wirelessly) and close any program that uses the web that you do not absolutely need, other than updating through your Internet provider.

Make sure your visitors are told to sit in a position with a good link and, if necessary, plug them directly into their router.

Trust in your ears and write notes

Trust in your ears is the bottom line and do not overthink it. Even though just about everyone initially hates the sound of their own voice, listening to anything you record is vital.

Follow your intuition when something sounds wrong when you replay the audio files.

As you create more episodes and start to like the final edit, each time you get behind the mic, take notes of the recording setup and work to imitate it.

Don't forget all about content

All for nothing is the cleanest, most professional sounding recording that does not contain interesting material. Don't hesitate to spend time on learning what makes a podcast episode fascinating, in addition to concentrating on your technique. Although new listeners can be turned off by an unpolished recording, a podcast that is not convincing can discourage even the most loyal fan.

Do not alienate the desire of your listeners to feel like they are involved by not acknowledging them in the podcast experience. If it is one-sided, it needs to be a mutually beneficial arrangement and will not function.

Highly active listeners who have an emotional bond with your podcast, listen more, inspire more, buy more, show more loyalty and become ambassadors of the brand.

8. EQUIPMENT, HARDWARE AND SOFTWARES FOR PODCASTING

One of the main factors to remember when scheduling a new show is podcast equipment. From mic to the mixer to recorder to machine, depending on how you record and catch your voice, the podcast equipment can be broken down into categories.

The method of recording can be as basic or as complex as you want. You can record your machine right away, get rid of the need for a mixer or a microphone, or you can go the full studio direction and use all four of them.

Hardware

Desk

A podcast desk is a platform that houses the computer, the microphone set and other voice recording devices for the modern media workplace. Podcast desks come in various sizes and configurations, for the single user or multiple guest.

Some podcast desk setup comes with build in-cable management and monitor arm positions to work with the ergonomics of the required setup.

Computers

After recording, the next piece of gear you are going to spend the rest of your time on is your computer. From importing files and editing audio/video to finally uploading the media online, this is where the magic takes place. For multiple functions such as recording, editing, computers with preinstalled applications can be used in podcasting.

There are indeed a variety of variables that play into your podcast or any device or laptop audio medium, and a lot of it depends on what DAW and plug-in software you are using (digital audio workstation or audio editing software).

Microphone

The microphone is essentially the instrument required to hear your voice and send it forward, making it the first component of our recording chain to be captured anywhere. It is worth noting that microphones come in many shapes, forms, and sizes as a main podcast unit.

1.   **Unidirectional Microphone**: The unidirectional microphone picks up sound from only one direction, primarily the direction in which it points. What makes unidirectional microphones a successful podcasting option is how they filter out ambient sounds by design, reproducing only the sound that is addressed to it. The best choice is unidirectional microphones for in-studio podcasting, interviews and quality recording.

2.   **Omnidirectional Microphone**: There are omnidirectional microphones that come pre-installed on laptops. They pick up sounds at once from all angles. Omnidirectional mics, along with background music, catch your sound.

3.   **Dynamic Microphone**: Dynamic microphone are microphones used for speaking in engagements and rock concerts. Most when someone mentions the word "microphone," the image that comes to mind is probably a dynamic microphone. These microphones function in reverse, like a speaker. This system sounds complicated, but the internal composition of dynamic microphones is such that a lot of incoming signal can be taken and audio is still clearly

produced. They are rugged in build so they can be manhandled.

4. **Condenser Microphone**: You may want to shop for studio condenser microphones when podcasting happens in the studio and you're searching for the subtleties and nuances of the human voice in your recording (the more detail you get, the better!). A condenser microphone's anatomy is somewhat different from that of a dynamic one. A diaphragm (similar to dynamics) is suspended in the condenser in front of a stationary plate conducting electricity. The air in between the diaphragm and the plate is displaced as a signal approaches the microphone, producing a fluctuating electrical charge.

The motion becomes an electrical representation of the incoming audio signal until provided a bit more power. You no longer need the audio card, the mixer, or any of the go-betweens once deemed necessary for connecting audio equipment to a device, the simple benefit of operating with USB microphones.

With USB condenser microphones, there is now a direct link to the device for the audio signal. It enables your production of podcasts extremely portable.

Microphone Boom Arm

A "boom arm" is fixed to the top of the stand so that the microphone in the horizontal plane can pass. When putting microphones on a desk stand, this can be especially useful when the microphone stands have to fight for space. In both fixed length and adjustable (telescoping) lengths, boom arms are provided.

XLR Cables

Cables are often used to connect the microphones to the audio interface, mixer, or pre-amp. In reality, there is a lot going into XLR microphone cables and cheap ones can trigger more issues than they are worth. For instance, a mid-range XLR cable is commonly recommended for beginners.

Headphones

A crucial part of the line-up of podcast equipment is headphones. There is a need for a fantastic set of podcast headphones with live podcasts to track the audio levels in real time and make quick changes to the audio interface or audio mixer. If an online interview show is being run, headphones are also required to listen to guests. They are useful for listening to recordings, and even for editing audio.

Camera

The best podcasting cameras are pretty much the same as those used for vlogging, but you can use any sort of camera that can capture 1080p videos However, because an upload of the video is needed on YouTube and other common video streaming sites such as Facebook, smartphone or webcam can also be used for video recording, it is important to make it look as good in terms of quality as most of the videos on there. Considering the recommended video quality, due to memory card recording limitations or the possibility of overheating the camera sensor, it may be difficult to use just any camera to capture long videos. Therefore, having an affordable camcorder or higher-end digital camera that supports long-form capture of video is critical. If you want to record more complex shots from the left and right of one or two hosts, using more than one camera is also a choice.

Storage media (such as USB Flash Drive/Memory Card/Backup Hard Drive)

The video camera to be used will obviously needs a memory card to record footage. Storage media such as USB Flash Drive, Memory Card, Hard Drive, provide a means of storing and creating a media back up for record content. It is always best to get the maximum memory card size that your camera will allow. A typical 64 GB memory card, will support about 40 minutes of video.

Tripod

Shooting from your own podcasting studio can require you to settle for any good tripod that can help your camera choice and achieve the desired height or level of shooting. If you're not going to take it outside or install heavy camera setups, there's no real need for a costly, high-quality tripod, but you can still use it if you already have one.

Audio Interface

An audio interface is important if you want high-quality audio, so we would still suggest using one for your live stream. The bridge between your microphone and your machine is essentially this. It transforms the mic's analog signal into a digital signal that can be used by the machine. I'm confident that you can easily find a way to link it to your device or video encoder to create a live podcast that sounds just as good as your audio podcasts.

Audio Mixer

Mono tracks and stereo tracks that can be used for the input or output of audio signals are provided by a mixing board. Mixing boards are outrageously flexible no matter the make or model. The only way to go when you and your friends crowd together to record is with several microphones.

The true benefit of the mixer is that it helps you to individually change the audio levels of those different inputs so that they sound even.

A mixer is only really necessary if you have more than one host, as with non-live video podcasts.

And it becomes much more important to use a hardware mixer while streaming live, which allows you to make careful adjustments in real time to each individual signal or channel, because there is no ability to go through post-production.

Compressor/Expander/EQ for My Mic and Interviews

A high-pass filter only makes it possible to pass through sounds above a certain frequency. Anything that is filtered out. No fundamental frequencies below about 85 Hz are created by most speaking voices, it is essential to determine a high-pass filter about 80-100 Hz to help suppress rumble and plosives that your listeners would never want to hear. A bit of equalization can help compensate for resonances in your room, or certain frequencies that might seem to stand out, when you hear your voice through your microphone. Generally, instead of raising them, it's easier to cut frequencies. Be wary of using drastic boosts or cuts of more than 6 dB. On your headphones or speakers, they can sound fine, but on a different set of headphones, they may be too serious.

Compression takes louder sounds and, if they happen, turns them down substantially, to even out the variations between loud and quiet words or parts. You can turn up the overall tone of your voice after compressing these quieter sounds, making it all seem louder overall.

This can be useful when in noisy conditions such as a subway, car, or bus, people listen to your podcast. Another effect which should not be used to extremes is this.

De-essing is like a combination of equalization and compression. This compresses your voice's pitch, but only in the frequency range where very sibilant (4-7 kHz) sounds live. When speaking into a microphone, the voices of several people show an awkward sibilant sound. A minor de-essing will make your voice simpler to listen to for a long period of time. Adjustments to the wide level will help get your podcast into a loudness range comparable to other podcasts.

Recorder

Speaking of digital recorders, to actually capture and store your audio, we need a podcast equipment option. This could be anything ranging from a computer, to a laptop, to a dedicated digital recorder itself. Anyone who wants to podcast on the go, but is aiming for a degree of sound quality above what is available for a smartphone, a dedicated digital recorder is a great choice.

On top of that, since they are simply made for recording, digital recorders provide a lot more settings and choices for producing audio. Since most of them come with built-in mics, you do not even need an extra mic to record into one.

In order to collect tons of fancy and pricey audio equipment, most individuals do not get into podcasting.

Instead of whether or not your long chain of gear is all working properly, it is easier to start simple so that you can concentrate on your real material. Over time, you can tweak and update stuff here and there as you expand. A podcast could host other materials for people interested in large equipment, such as mic activator, mix pre stand, direct input box, power conditioner, rack, studio monitors (2x), desktop stands (2x) monitor, floor stands (2x) monitor, subwoofer, subwoofer stand, controller/headphone amp monitor, sound screen, rechargeable aa batteries + adapter, air sign, surge protector, power supply backup.

Software

Depending on the task to be achieved, various software packages are used for podcasting. Below are two different categories of typical software used:

- Video Recording/Editing Software

Non-live podcasts offer the option, both in terms of your audio and video, of getting more control over what you air. You get the ability to combine your video and audio files, make cuts, change your audio levels, and more. First do the video and then export it twice, as an audio-video file and for upload on common podcast platforms as an audio-only file. Another approach to shorten and reduce the workflow is to directly record your video and audio into your app. You can attach your camera and microphone to your device with free video editing apps, such as Windows Movie Maker and iMovie, so you can edit your files directly after capturing them. A list of video recording options and tools are given below:

Primary Camera + Webcam: Canon EOS R with Sigma 24mm Art Lens

Lens Adapter: Canon Mount Adapter EF-EOS R

Camera Mount System: Watch the Video Example and Tutorial

Video Capture Card: Cam Link 4k

Secondary Webcam: Logitech BRIO 4k

Video Hosting: YouTube and Teachable

Quick Video Communication: Loom

Convert Podcast Audio to YouTube Videos: Repurpose

Video Editing and Screen Recording: Screen Flow

Shotgun Microphone: Sennheiser ME66/K6

Lavalier Microphone: Tram TR50

Field Recorder: Zoom F2-BT

Lights: Cowboy Studio

Collapsible Background: Fotodiox Background Panel

Podcasting Software & Online Tools

Popular podcast editing software are Audacity or Garageband. They are both free and relatively easy to use and learn. A list of podcasting software & online tools are given below:

Podcast Hosting + Dynamic Ad Insertion: Megaphone

RSS Feed: FeedPress

Ad-Free Podcast Hosting: Patreon

DAW (Digital Audio Workstation): Adobe Audition CC

Audio Editing/Cleanup: iZotope RX8 Auditor Editor (Standard Edition)

WAV File Utility (to split 32-Bit Float Poly WAV Files): AudioMove

Audio Cart (for playing live music & sound effects): Podcast Soundboard

Audio Tagging: ID3 Tag Editor

Scheduling Interviews: Acuity Scheduling

Theme Music: iStock Audio + YouTube Audio Library + Storyblocks

Internet Interviews: Cleanfeed Pro

Optimize Internet Data during Recordings: TripMode

Convert Podcast Audio to YouTube Videos: Repurpose

Internet Connection

You can easily link to the web and upload your video podcast at your own ease once all the editing, exporting, and meta-tagging is completed.

Publishing a Podcast

Publishing is everything that happens after the final audio files has been produced. It includes creating the episode page, adding show notes, uploading your media file and any promotion required for the episode. ITunes, Google podcast, Stitcher, Spotify and TuneIn are some of the common names where variety of podcast topics relating to technology, health fitness, personal finance, news, sports, music, politics and so on. It is a fairly common misconception that iTunes (now Apple Podcasts) and other podcast directories host a podcast media files. Podcast episode files are not actually uploaded to iTunes rather via an RSS feed, iTunes is shown the location of the podcast files recorded.

You should end up with what is called an RSS feed, which includes a list of your podcast episodes and all their details to be interpreted by directories and other apps, no matter what podcast host you select. Depending on your podcast host, the means of adding this information to your RSS feed will differ, but it will usually consist of:

Name

This one is straightforward! As described, you should try to choose a name that is impactful, that has not yet been used by someone else, and explain what your podcast is about. For guidance and to prevent any collisions, look at other podcasts on Apple Podcasts or another list. As part of the title, you can always add a brief summary if you believe this will help.

Description

Usually, you would have space for a more comprehensive overview of your podcast. This would usually take the form of a summary of the fundamental contents and format, the hosts and any frequent guests. You will also have space for a summary customized to every single episode that you upload.

Categories

Categories are included in iTunes and other repositories, which help people locate podcasts based on their interests. At least one category that is specifically related to the content of your podcast should be selected, but you may also choose subcategories that relate to more peripheral elements.

Rating

In other words, if they include swear words, you will also have to let iTunes know whether your podcast episodes are 'clean' or 'explicit.' It is debatable that clean podcasts have a greater potential audience - and often in the iTunes interface they are more heavily advertised - but this is not something you should care about in particular.

Artwork

The trick to getting individuals interested in your podcast is great cover art. Alongside your podcast feed, your podcast artwork will appear, and also (by default) any podcast that the listener downloads to their smartphone.

This is both a marketing tool and something that people can see each week (or upload as much as you do), so you want it to look nice and show all that your podcast stands for. Although opting for something creative is great, several podcasts prefer to include the name in the artwork prominently. This is helpful in identifying it in apps that sort your podcasts by tiles, particularly when you need to scroll through a lot of podcasts. Make sure it's bold and fills the frame either way, as people can see it as both a tiny thumbnail and an 'album artwork' that fills the entire screen of their phone.

The artwork itself should have a minimum of 1400x1400 pixels and a maximum resolution of 2048x2048.

This is the scale acknowledged by Apple Podcasts, which continues to be the biggest online podcast index. This will be approved by all podcast players (podcatchers) and means that your artwork on high and low resolution devices will look equally fine.

Some podcatchers also allow the use of a different picture for each individual podcast episode. Although some podcasts stick to the same image, others use this as an excuse to use a thematic image, such as a still from the TV episode they are reviewing, or a special piece of artwork based on the episode. This is not necessary (and could be a copyright grey area), but it is something to consider going forward.

Here is a list of steps recommended to upload your podcast files.

1. Podcast episodes are uploaded in the form of an .mp3 file to your podcast host.

2. It is recommended to publish show notes with links to resources mentioned in the episode, a summary of what was discussed, and/or a transcript of the show hosted.

3. Submit your podcast RSS Feed to iTunes or other directories.

Note: Firstly, it is crucial to highlight that Apple Podcasts (iTunes) are used by many directories and most podcast listening apps as their source of podcast data. This means that after an upload to iTunes, t podcast will automatically show up in apps like Overcast, Castbox, and Pocket Casts.

9. MONETIZING YOUR PODCAST: HOW TO MAKE YOUR PODCAST PROFITABLE (TIPS AND TRICKS FOR MONETIZING YOUR NEW PODCAST)

Remember the good old days where a podcast is launched without thought of how to recover (and exceed) your time and money commitment. Your monetization plan should be top of mind from the start, whether you produce revenue from advertising and sponsorships or use the show to raise authority and attract new customers.

There are various ways of monetizing a podcast. There isn't a clear direction or a perfect way to do it.

However, the trick is to monetize your podcast in a manner that doesn't deceive your listeners. This means discovering a strategy of monetization that they do not find intrusive. In several instances, rather than pushing one technique too far, that means using a little bit of many techniques.

Podcast Monetization

A long-term plan that can produce revenue in a number of ways is to launch a podcast. When we speak about monetizing a podcast, we don't restrict the debate to specifically generating revenue from ad sales on the podcast. Leveraging a podcast requires every possible opportunity for revenue-making that comes from hosting the broadcast. The importance of getting authority in the eyes of a captive, committed audience; or, yes, direct ad and sponsorship income built into the show may be sales made to leads who learn about you from the show.

The running of podcasts costs money. You'll incur costs along the way, whether you're a hobbyist, a professional trying to establish authority, or starting a company based on podcasting. You set yourself sustainable for the long run when you prepare your monetization strategy early on in the process.

Without it being a huge money pit, you can launch and expand your show. It's important to position your show for monetization as soon as possible if you're taking your podcast seriously. There are two primary reasons why:

1. The manufacturing expense

It takes money and time to make a show, so you would probably want something in exchange. Even if the aim of starting a podcast isn't to make money, running the show would still cost money. Owing to an unlimited abundance in today's economy, material is ultimately worthless. An intrinsic zero content value implies that in the ecosystem developed around that content, the only real value is.

2. It's expensive to create an audience and expand distribution. Monetization assists to relieve the effort.

Even if making money is not your primary objective, monetization is still essential to your audience's understanding and development. The monetization method is about recognizing the importance of your audience first and foremost.

Niching Down

Niche down every time when creating an audience. That strategy is how you end up trapped just being able to sell ads. We never suggest targeting the mass market.

Most shows will never be huge. You should expect that, per episode, your show will never have more than 10,000 listeners.

In several cases, 3,000 listeners will not break even. It's still a significant audience, and that's OK. Think about it in these terms: What is the highest number of people you've talked to at a meeting or function in front of a live event? That number is less than 700 for most individuals who aren't keynote speakers. And it's likely less than 175 really.

If your podcast splits each episode with your live speaking max number, it's like getting your life's biggest speaking gig every week.

Even when a show may have only a couple of hundred listeners per episode, you should be assured that a high-value audience is tuning in when you niche down. Getting a small number of focused, high-value listeners is better than hundreds of people who are not your target audience.

The next move is to understand your choices for various methods of monetization once you've done your consumer research and established your high-value audience segments. You need to know how each choice works and for which types of shows before you select which route is right for you.

Sponsorships do not rely on the action taken by your audience, but they depend more heavily on the importance of your audience to the sponsor. Typically, sponsorship deals include a fixed price and do not necessarily require an ad in the broadcast, but you need to settle on a way to let the viewer's know that the show is sponsored by a specific organization.

A show ought to have a specific number of packages to sell for sponsorship. In a regular or annual basis, they could be offered or you could have one sponsor on an ongoing basis.

Should one start a podcast to generate income?

While podcast revenue is on the rise, it is not advisable to start a podcast solely to generate income.

Getting a loyal audience is the basis of how to earn money when podcasting. Loyal viewers follow hosts who have a passion for their subject matter.

There would be a noticeable lack of excitement and, in turn, no excited listeners tuning in each week if the sole purpose of a podcast is to earn money.

Begin a podcast because you want to share with the world your distinctive voice, not because you want to make some easy money.

But note, don't make money using your listeners. Rather, build genuine relationships with your listeners and make money using those relationships. There is a gap there. When you're being pretentious, people know.

The techniques which are currently the most common fall into the category of direct monetization. When the show is the thing you're offering, direct podcast monetization is. You will benefit from creating original content, repurposing it, and giving paying members exclusive access.

There's indirect podcast monetization on the other hand. And that is when you sell other items using your podcast as a tool. Your podcast is a medium for promoting goods and creating demand among your audience

Collaborations

Partnerships are much like steroid sponsorships. Joint projects, broad cross-promotions, tournaments, or even a takeover of the social partnership could be collaborations.

Accounts for the media. You become an evangelist for their product when you collaborate with others, and them for theirs.

Partnerships also require the exchange of marketing knowledge, such as the cross-installation of a retargeting pixel, so that partners can directly target show listeners.

A hypothetical scenario: Let's say you run an adventure show based on hiking, camping, fishing, and other travel experiences. To give your audience an adventure package, you could partner with a travel company and an outdoor gear company. Your partners get listed when you advertise the contest in your show. And your partners will share the contest and link in your podcast with their audience.

It makes the deal mutually beneficial, especially if you both have broad audiences within a common niche consisting of numerous individuals. If executed well, this partnership opportunity could turn into a long-term arrangement.

The easiest way to win partnership deals is to reach individuals or brands in your sector one-on-one, which you think will be a good match for a partnership.

Brands will often reach out with opportunities, but you will have to put in the effort on research and outreach if you want to take collaborations seriously.

It is important to bear in mind that collaborations are highly tailored to maximize the advantages that each party can bring to each other. Place yourself as someone who can bring value to them and their audience while you are recruiting a potential partner. The more meaning you can add, the greater the likelihood that a better relationship can be achieved.

Request for donations

Asking individuals for money is the best way to monetize a podcast. Many fans are willing to throw their favourite podcasters a couple of dollars to ensure that they continue to get great material. This is always the first approach that is suggested when people ask how to monetize a podcast, since it's simple to set up and support.

Many models of premium content are sold as gifts, where you can pick how much you donate and receive exclusive content in exchange. The least you can do if you are considering asking for donations is create premium content for the individuals who send you donations. Your content ought to be good enough that people want to pay for it, while donations could work.

If people pay for it, you have a great chance to switch into another model, such as premium content or a subscription system.

Keep the calls-to-action genuine to stop feeling stinky about this form of self-promotion. Are you calling for donations to make new episodes so you can spend more time? Say that to your audience. They'll be more likely to donate if people understand where the money is going.

Play around with the level choices if you go with Patreon. With gifts, material, or other perks, you can thank fans for their support. You will find that more listeners are likely to support the show because, for their donation, they receive either a tangible object or exclusive episodes or even a shout out.

Guests Charging

A huge number of people seem to be against charging guests in the podcast industry. But if the audience is to the point where visitors are prepared to pay for the publicity, charge them for a spot on the show by all means. People who would pay to appear on a podcast, or people wanting to get their name out, are likely to already have their own brand to advertise. The podcast interview, a blog post, and social promotion can include a guest kit.

Offer sponsorships or commercials

The most popular method of monetizing a podcast is sponsorship. It's also the simplest, aside from taking gifts, because you don't have to build or sell something. Everything you need to do is set up a sponsor deal.

You would have probably heard podcasters beginning their show or breaking in with something like "[some company] brings this episode to you." This is sponsorship. Depending on how many individuals listen to your show, sponsorships cost more. If the number of people listening increases, the income will rise as well. But this also means that if you do not have many listeners, this is a difficult way to make money. You will usually charge for references to "pre-roll" and "semi-roll." Pay more in mid-row (during your episode). At all points, support the sponsor if you're pleased.

Join a network of advertisements

As intermediaries between hosts and advertisers, advertising networks such as Midroll, AdvertiseCast, Podcorn, and PodGrid run.

They'll take a cut from the ad placements included in your show when you apply for each platform. So make sure you're reading the fine print. The revenue share usually follows a CPM model where you are paid for every 1,000 ad unit impressions received.

Sell episodes for value

There's a fair chance that some of them will opt for premium versions of your content because you know your audience wants to listen to your podcast. All you have to do is make some exclusive recordings that are available for purchase only.

You may consider selling:

- Questions and Answers with exclusive guests
- Early access to episodes that will one day be online
- Ad-free episodes
- Episodes live-streamed

Your Back Catalogue Gate

Try this approach if you started a podcast ages ago and have developed a back catalogue of episodes. You can limit access to your older shows, instead of creating new premium content. This means that a paywall for users will be added to listen to the older content.

Recording it when you record your free stuff is a simple way to create premium content. Let's just say you're inviting a guest to your show. Record a conversation for 30 minutes, then an extra 10 minutes to sell as a bonus. Make sure that there is something juicy that customers want to buy for an additional 10 minutes.

A note of warning here: Make sure your free stuff still has plenty of value. You don't want your listeners to think that you're hiding all the positive things in the paid material, or they're not going to bother you.

Sell material that is recycled

To recycle items you have already created is a perfect way to make sellable content. This decreases the amount of time you spend making something similar.

Take a couple of your best episodes of the podcast that apply to related subjects. Right from your screen, transcribe them yourself or use Castos automatic transcription services.

Then edit the transcripts, add more meaning and money anywhere you can, and bring them into a book together.

If your listeners appeal to this technique to monetize a podcast, spend a little money from platforms like 99Designs into a skilled design. So you can put it in a format that is appropriate like amazon.

It is much more convenient to sell books on Amazon than to try to sell them on your own website.

First, on your podcast, market your latest book. Figure out that what you've taught is a thorough way to learn. And that is when you sell other items using your podcast as a tool. Your podcast is a medium for promoting goods and creating demand among your audience.

Each technique of monetization involves its own collection of abilities and expertise that takes time to learn and comprehend. Since you have never sold physical products before, for instance, your podcast may not have been a good first try. You need to have the experience to effectively sell a tangible product.

Publishing your podcasts on YouTube

Publishing your podcasts on YouTube as videos is a simple way to squeeze some money out of what you've already made.

It's a smooth process here. All you should do is allow your account settings to be monetized, and Google will handle the ads and distribute your money.

How much are you going to make on YouTube? It depends on a variety of variables, such as video views, how long people watch, whether your ads are missed, and whether your ads are clicked on.5 You will make between $0.50 and $1.55 per view, generally speaking.

Split it into consumable chunks that last three to five minutes, rather than simply uploading the entire video. For example, a few vibe questions from your interview could be sliced out. You will end up with more video material even though it all comes from the same recording. Then give it a convincing headline that will make individuals want to click.

Premium Content and Subscriptions

The purest type of monetization is subscriptions, with your audience directly supporting your imagination and media.

This would mean that a strong connection can be seen between your subscriptions and how pleased your general audience is. Your subscribers are an exceptional predictor of how satisfied your audience is.

It means you're doing a good job if they're able to pay for more. Subscription monetization, also referred to as premium content, includes continuity, dedication, and continuous execution. They will expect exclusive content on a fixed schedule if anyone pays a monthly fee to access premium content, or they will terminate their subscription. Subscriptions are an excellent way to monetize the scale of a house.

You need to take time to learn what's considered premium content for your market in order for a subscription model to be viable. If a market is already very saturated, it will not be enough to produce the same form of content, just twice, to gain subscribers. In this same case, an elevated edition of your free content, not a mirror image, should be your unique content.

How to Indirectly Monetize a Podcast

Here are many more ways for your podcast to make money. Here are some methods for indirectly monetizing a podcast.

Sell goods for physical use

They could be purchasing merchandise that shows off the show if an audience likes a podcast. Outside of making the latest shows, you might sell T-shirts, mugs, stickers, or something that really lets your audience interact with the show. Showcase the name of the podcast, a repeated catch phrase, or the merchant's inner joke. The moment a listener can pass a stranger on the street and realize they're wearing a tee shirt from their favourite show can be defined by your calls-to-action. A connection is created instantly out of their mutual love for your show.

Public Speaking

For a lot of podcast hosts, public speaking is simply an easy transition. You will probably do better in front of an audience if you are comfortable talking at your show. Apparently, standing in front of a bunch of people is a specific challenge, but if you already know how to write a script, it is indeed less of a concern.

It varies greatly as to how much you can make on speaking fees. Some speakers get a small stipend and expenses for travel. Six figures or more are rendered by other speakers.

How do you get into speaking in public?

- To discuss your niche or business, find local groups that meet. Try Meet up, Facebook groups, or even the source that organizes the event in your local paper.

- Contact them and propose a topic to present, but be open to their suggestions for subjects. Let them know that you intend to have your podcast plugged in.

- Build a visual presentation and outline a script. In the meantime, you would have to start small. Don't expect stadiums or even auditoriums to be full. Your first speaking session might be attended by 5-10 people, but that's all right. Use those gigs to sharpen your presentation skills and develop relationships.

Sell slots for masterminds

As you get more meaning from it than just money, a mastermind community is a unique way to monetize a podcast. A mastermind is a small minority of people who are committed to supporting each other for a common cause. They provide education, brainstorming, and openness to help you stay on track with whatever you're trying to learn or achieve.

For limited, high-value audiences, masterminds and private communities work well. You just need a few hundred committed listeners to start a mastermind, maybe even less. In general, a mastermind consists of 8 to 12 individuals who are involved in growing together. To form a mastermind, you don't need many individuals; the small size holds the value per person high.

Even if you only have 400 listeners, you can try to get a mastermind started. It's possible that most of your listeners are interested in similar types of growth opportunities and will learn a lot from each other if you have developed a niche audience. For mastermind memberships, especially if you have a B2B or other high-value audience, you might charge between $7,000 and $25,000.

Some podcasters utilize masterminds and communities as their primary source of monetization so they can focus on making the material as good as possible and the revenue is large enough.

Masterminds pair well with selling services, particularly for coaches who provide one-on-one services as well as a community mastermind.

Even though you have 400 listeners, you can try to get a mastermind started. It's possible that most of your listeners are interested in similar types of growth opportunities and will learn a lot from each other if you have developed a niche audience. For mastermind memberships, specifically if you have a B2B or other high-value audience, you might charge between $7,000 and $25,000.

Offer goods from affiliates

Certain businesses have open partner services that you can take advantage of. There's no need for you to negotiate a deal or get accepted. You just sign up and tell them where your payments should be sent. Whenever anyone signs in with your link, you get paid.

You might sell other people's goods for a share of their profits instead of making your own products to sell.

To do this, there are two strategies:

The first strategy is to self-promote their goods. Audible's partner program is popular among podcasters, for instance. They give you a free promotion link. Anytime anyone signs up for a free trial using your link, you earn up more than $15. The second strategy is to make the creator of the product come to your show to sell their own items. The advantage here is that the owner of the product knows better than you how to market his own product, then they can say the correct things to generate further sales.

Generate leads for business

In order to fund broader projects, several organizations launch podcasts.

You're in the perfect place to generate extremely qualified leads if you host a podcast that enhances your company. For instance, claim you own an accounting firm and recently started a podcast to educate people about how to pay their taxes. As you give free advice on the show, you also weave in the importance of your business to tax people for them.

Offer facilities for consultation or coaching

The greatest advantage of hosting a podcast is that you build yourself in a niche as an expert. As an educated professional, the audience is here to respect you. So providing services that fit in with your subject is a perfect way to monetize a podcast. For example, personal life coaching might be provided by a productivity and wellness podcast. An advertising podcast could sell marketing strategies that are customized.

It is pretty quick to get started here. For people to sign up for a coaching session with you, you only need a landing page on your website with a form or widget.

What's a session for coaching? Anything you want can be that. It may be as easy as a phone call or Skype chat, or as complicated as a visit to the location of the client in person. Put together some sort of service that is right for your client.

Selling an App

If you are acutely aware of the difficulties and problems of your audience, by creating an app that fits their needs, you can monetize a podcast. You could offer a calendar app tailored especially for parents if you host a parenting podcast. You could sell a bright star finder app if you host an astronomy podcast. Conversely, you might sell a simple branded app that helps individuals better connect with you and your content. It could have episodes of your podcast, blog content, notes, your schedule, and maybe a way to speak directly with you.

Production of software can be costly if you do not really know how to go about it yourself. Before you get started, make sure that you get a lot of details from a developer so that you don't burn too much money or end up with a half-finished product you can't afford.

Launch a network of podcasts

Some hosts want to be part of a podcast network, while others like their autonomy. But a network's one advantage is bargaining power.

The relative control that someone has over someone else is bargaining power. When each side has reasonably equal bargaining power, within a negotiation, each has the same footing.

You're positioning your podcast and others to have more fair power to the advertisers you want to draw by creating a podcast network.

It may take several forms to start a podcast network and be either a structured, contractual framework or something more DIY. Team up in your niche with complementary shows where you have some overlap or build a network full of unrelated shows to target various niches. In either case, pooling each podcast's scope and power within a network helps you to pitch more lucrative sponsorship deals. As you have improved your bargaining power, you also have more of a chance to get on the radar of larger advertisers with bigger budgets.

The networking opportunities it provides are one of the often-overlooked advantages of a podcast. Although the ties made by podcasting are not direct income, they are just one step away. Some common ways in which content-based networking can lead to revenue through a podcast include:

-For consultancy and service sales, communicating with and warming up prospects and leads.

-Increased keynote and other possibilities for speech.

-Encouraging connections for future collaborations.

-Growing the power to work for book deals and other related possibilities.

-Building very good interactions within your business.

The monetary value of relationships cannot, and should not, be calculated directly. But know that in the bigger ones, every relationship you establish and develop through podcasting (and pertinent activities) is significant.

Indirect method of generating money in podcasting

These includes:

Sell an e-course for exposure

If your podcast is educational or intends to teach a new skill to listeners, the ideal way to earn some cash is to build a solo e-course.

You can even do it on your own website (with a tool such as MemberPress) or host it all on a third-party platform such as Udemy, Coursera, or Skillshare to build a course.

Offer information products

An information resource is a type of content that people buy to learn new things. It could be anything: a prototype, a guide, an eBook, a worksheet, a resource, etc. A general knowledge product would not have to apply to a single show, unlike content upgrades, but can address a larger issue or problem faced by your listeners. The biggest advantage of selling information items through your podcast is that you can plug them into your podcast script as much as you want to keep sales from falling flat. You can also source your listeners' questions or feedback and respond to them on your show, which brings more value to their order.

Hosting an event

Sell tickets to a live event where you can be greeted in person by your fans if you have a local follower or a devout audience who wouldn't mind traveling to see you.

Your audience and the topic of your podcast will depend on the type of event you are hosting. You may give a lecture, hold a workshop, teach a skill, or simply host a group discussion.

This is a hard way for a podcast to be monetized, to be honest. Until you have a loyal following, it would be better to hold on to this idea. To turn a profit, events don't need thousands of attendees, because you need some people to turn up.

That type of exposure would help companies within their niche, and the targeted audience gives them a better chance of earning a strong ROI.

To make them effective, events often require a lot of prior knowledge and planning. If you have never scheduled a large-scale event before, then you're probably going to spend a lot of time and money finding out how to do it. To run the event for you, you might employ an event planner or team, which may cost just as much for an event that might yet not be profitable.

Over time, activities tend to become more successful, so controlling the expectations when deciding to monetize events is important.

Sell Updated Content

Including a downloadable resource with each podcast episode that applies to that episode is a clever way to monetise a podcast. This is called an enhancement of content because it updates or improves the experience of the listener. You will have to put a payment form on your web somewhere for listeners to pay and download the form in order to offer a content update. The most suitable place for this is the page on which you post your podcast download links and/or audio player.

And if you sell content upgrades to monetize a podcast, you can add an e-commerce shopping cart to your website so that you can individually list your content upgrades. This way, rather than sorting through every post, people can search your previous upgrades in one place.

Coaching

A podcast is also used by coaches and consultants as a central marketing channel. Unless you're a coach or consultant hosting a podcast, from day one, you can begin talking about your services. This does not mean selling every episode to your viewers, but merely sending the message that this is what you are doing for a living.

Costs

When preparing your podcast, there are two forms of costs you can determine. First is how much it costs for the show to be made. Second is how much the implementation of your monetization path would cost.

To deliver a show people want to listen to, you need to be able to spend money and/or time. Consider the expense of implementation when considering alternative monetization paths.

A small incident can indeed be costly to put on, and holding a series of conferences is even more costly. It gets harder over time to handle and sell a collection of live recordings. The cost of research is relatively small, but the cost of implementing it is huge.

Other channels of monetization would be more costly to evaluate up front, but have a lower long-term cost of implementation. Stuff such as online classes and courses are an instance where you would have higher upfront costs to manufacture the goods and test the market. When you find out those stuff, they are cost-effective in long-term maintenance and profitability.

Why some Podcasts flop

It is the nature of the format that podcasts evolve at a slower pace than other media. Building an audience on a podcast takes time because a podcast is cultivated rather than anything else by word of mouth referrals several times. Even if it's on a growth track, so long as you keep putting out good material, it will keep growing.

Podcasts are a slower platform, but with an audience, they create deeper relationships. Find out why if you have a podcast listener, and they're not buying from you. If they listen, it implies they are pretty committed to your brand already. Shows that don't monetize seem to be either artistic hobby shows or hosts who may not want to make money. These shows collapse because the cost of production (time or money) would inevitably exceed the motivation of the host to keep the show running.

Thank you for reading This Book.

If you enjoyed it please visit the site where you purchased it and write a brief review.

Your feedback is important to me and will help other readers decide wheter to read the book too.

Thank you!

David Toll

www.ingramcontent.com/pod-product-compliance
Lightning Source LLC
Chambersburg PA
CBHW071242050326
40690CB00011B/2227